"There is a Hamlet in each of us—troubled hours where we are called to choose and yet flee that appointment. In The Art of Decision Making, Joseph Bikart explores the anatomy of this perpetual dilemma: which factors lead to choice, and which keep us from choosing? Bikart leads the reader to greater understanding, greater accountability, and greater facility in cutting through the nettlesome thicket of life to a place of resolve."

James Hollis, Ph.D, psychoanalyst and bestselling author of Living an Examined Life

"Joseph Bikart's The Art of Decision Making is volatile. It shakes you by the scruff of your procrastination and wilfully wakes you from your slumber of indecision. As Eliot's Prufrock soberly reminds us, every decision, even trouser leg style, has within it the potential to activate agony.

Navigating the complex world of how we decide or more urgently, how we avoid decision, is for many of us, a stormy sea. Bikart steers a brilliant course through these difficult waters and delivers his reader to new and clear-blue depths, encompassing the philosophy, psychology and cartography of every dimension of decision making. The best decision you will make today will be to clear your decks, inner and outer, and create space to devour this feast of wisdom. By turns erudite, creative, demanding, challenging, practical and insightful, The Art of Decision Making is blissfully relieving of the haunting tension of messy, clumsy and incompetent deciding."

Martin Lloyd-Elliott, Chartered psychologist, psychotherapist, business coach and bestselling author

"On this journey of self-discovery, Joseph Bikart starts quietly, asking at first why we struggle with decisions and inviting us to listen to our own answers; with increasing intensity, he guides us further into our selves, revealing the opportunities that decisions can represent in our lives; and by the end, he reaches a thundering crescendo in which he summons the power of the will to transform the world! No wonder that he can work magic for his clients, of whom I am proud to be one."

Hugh Verrier, chairman of the global law firm White & Case

Joseph Bikart is a founding partner and director of the international consulting firm Templar Advisors. For the past 20 years, following a first career in investment banking, he has advised leaders in corporate and public life on their communication and negotiations. Through his work with thousands of decision-makers, he has created *Decisiology*, an innovative approach to executive coaching, drawing on his studies at the Institute of Psychoanalysis and at the Tavistock in London. He is also a keynote speaker, and a lecturer at the London Business School and he holds a master's degree (hons) from ESCP Europe.

The Art of Decision Making

Joseph Bikart

The Art of Decision Making

How We Move from Indecision to Smart Choices

WATKINS

Sharing Wisdom Since 1893

This edition first published in the UK and USA 2019 by
Watkins, an imprint of Watkins Media Limited
Unit 11, Shepperton House
89-93 Shepperton Road
London
N1 3DF

enquiries@watkinspublishing.com

Design and typography copyright © Watkins Media Limited 2019

Text copyright © Joseph Bikart 2019

1 3 5 7 9 10 8 6 4 2

Typeset by Integra Software Services Pvt. Ltd, Pondicherry

Printed and bound in the China

A CIP record for this book is available from the British Library

ISBN: 978-1-78678-361-5

www.watkinspublishing.com

NOTES TO THE READER

This book presents a continuous argument, and is best read in its entirety. However, as on any long journey, signage can be helpful here and there. The occasional Orientation Points underline some of the main points of the thesis in everyday language related to practical decision making. They are tips, for easy consumption.

In addition, the book includes six Key Skills essays, contributed by lifestyle writer Mike Annesley. These are intended to offer practical decision-making guidelines consistent with the argument of the main text. They should be seen as *complementing or counterpointing* the main text, from a less philosophical perspective, rather than straightforwardly illustrating it. The essays are positioned to reflect some of the broad points made in the chapters that precede them. Each essay is headed with a relevant quotation from the book, with a page reference.

ACKNOWLEDGEMENTS

Thanks are due to:

– Martin Lloyd-Elliott for encouraging me to write this book, and for his unfailing and generous support

– James Hollis for inspiring me to write in the first place, and for his enlightening wisdom

– everyone at Templar Advisors, the dream team I feel blessed to work with every day

– the friends, relatives, clients and colleagues whose advice and feedback have been invaluable: Antti Ilmanen, Malka Napchan, Katherine Green, Jessica Jackson, Simon Eagles, Michael Knipe, Wylie O'Sullivan, Isabelle Bikart, Reyne Kérob, Paula Kérob, Ruth Goetz, Hugo Jackson, Pierre Morgan-Davies, James Patrick, Russell Ross-Smith, Johnny Ryan, Donna Fischetto, Adrien Mastrosimone, Stéphane Ducroizet, Cyrille Jaman, Leo Rom, Daniela Shayo, Hugh Verrier, Mikki Mahan, Monique Villa, Andrea Kracht, Neil Mackinnon, Suzanne Hull, Virginie Puertolas-Syn, Chloé Ducroizet-Boitaud, Nicola Foster, Sébastien Desprez, Alexandre Rieunier, Justine Smith, Anne Longfield, Vanessa Garet, Quentin Besnard, Thierry Morel, Damian Alexander

– my agent, Cathryn Summerhayes at Curtis Brown

– my publisher, Jo Lal at Watkins and her team, with special thanks to Bob Saxton.

Finally, most of all thanks to my parents, to whom it would take an entire book to express my deep gratitude, love and respect.

CONTENTS

Prologue   *1*

Introduction   5

PART I   INDECISION, INDECISION   11

Chapter 1   Paradise Lost   13

Chapter 2   Defence Forces   19

Chapter 3   Project Fear   27

Chapter 4   Through the Looking Glass   57
Key skill 1:   *How to manage risk*   61
Key skill 2:   *How to attain detachment*   63

PART II   WHERE ART THOU?   67

Chapter 5   Self Starters   69

Chapter 6   Hidden Chambers   73
Key skill 3:   *How to use intuition*   96

PART III THE MOMENTUM OF DECISIVENESS *99*

Chapter 7 Of the Essence *101*

Chapter 8 Decision Flow *105*

Chapter 9 Under the Hood *109*
Key skill 4: *How to accept the unchangeable and change the unacceptable* *117*

PART IV THE DECIDING MIND *121*

Chapter 10 A Question of Perspective *123*

Chapter 11 The Thread Between Our Decisions *149*

Chapter 12 Engaging with the Flow of the Will *153*

Chapter 13 Our Narrative *161*

Chapter 14 Mind Your Language *167*
Key skill 5: *How to decide under pressure* *177*

Conclusion *179*

Epilogue *183*

Endnotes *189*

PROLOGUE

"Human freedom involves our capacity to pause between stimulus and response and, in that pause, to choose the one response toward which we wish to throw our weight."

Rollo May, psychologist

Where you are today, in your personal and professional life, is the result of decisions you once made. Where you will be in the future depends on the decisions you are about to take.

Various aspects of our lives seem to escape this reality. Our health, for example, is strongly influenced by our genetic make-up. But it also depends on our lifestyle choices, such as the foods we eat or the exercise we take.

Sometimes our path is interrupted by fate. We are sidetracked away from our chosen road. But even then, it is our response to such events, more than the events themselves, that shapes our destiny.

Every facet of your life depends on the decisions you take. Yet how often do you pause to reflect on your ability to make smart choices? If your answer is "not enough", you are in good company.

When I first told my friends and clients I was writing a book on decisions, the news provoked two types of reaction:

"I desperately need this. Please hurry up!"

or this variation:

"I know someone who really needs this" (generally referring to a husband, wife, colleague, boss, son-in-law or the like).

We all face challenging decisions from time to time, even though their frequency and intensity may differ. This is not an admission of weakness or inadequacy. On the contrary, these moments indicate we are in the right place. They are a sign that we are engaged in a process that can be unsettling but can also stretch us and help us to grow. A world without challenging decisions would be terribly dull and stale.

The real question is not *whether* we face such choices, but *how*. This is the territory we'll explore together.

This book is about human volition – volition being "the power to use one's own will in order to make decisions".

The link between *will* and *decision* is well established. We find it in the expression, "Where there's a will, there's a way," as well as its French equivalent, "*Vouloir, c'est pouvoir*" ("If you will, you can"). But we also know that we sometimes stumble, that the link may be broken, and that however much we want something, we can find it hard to transform our will into action.

As a result, we end up with a list of unrealized dreams, a repository of regrets, which makes us question our own ability to take important decisions.

The Art of Decision Making aims to explore and restore volition. My mission in this book is to sketch out the roadmap that takes us from will to action.

This is not your traditional self-help manual. Bookshops and internet sites are full of such material that promises to transform us, rid us of our fears, make us more likeable, successful, emotionally intelligent, thinner, healthier, and so on.

You will not find here a series of pre-canned answers. Instead, you will be asked the right questions. In this respect, the book is *heuristic*, a term which comes from the Greek word for "discovery". My aim is to help you discover the answers, which means, first, addressing questions that will make you think, react and change. As the poet Rainer Maria Rilke wrote in his *Letters to a Young Poet*:

> "Be patient toward all that is unsolved in your heart and try to love the *questions themselves*, like locked rooms and like books that are now written in a very foreign tongue. Do not now seek the answers, which cannot be given you because you would not be able to live them. And the point is, to live everything. *Live* the questions now. Perhaps you will then gradually, without noticing it, live along some distant day into the answer."

The Art of Decision Making is not only for people who struggle with their decisions. Not everybody has the same pain threshold when it comes to making difficult choices. However, irrespective of how marginally or excruciatingly difficult we find decision making, the quest is the same, and in turn the approach taken and the tools used will be the same.

The book is also for people who do not encounter difficulties when *making* decisions, but may find it hard to live with their outcomes.

And finally, it may even be for people who do not experience any problems at all, but sense that the quality of their decision making has a great influence on their lives and careers. Recent research shows that "acting decisively" is the second most important contributor to the quality known as "executive presence". When people perceive us as decisive, they are more likely to listen to us and to follow us.

As for the question of what decisions are covered by this book, the answer is simple: it is those decisions that matter to you. Whether it is career change, choice of partner (or the decision to go separate ways), or even coping with the middle-age malaise of "having made all the wrong decisions" … the list is endless, reflecting the multiplicity of our wishes and aspirations.

The Art of Decision Making outlines the approach behind *Decisiology*, a methodology I have developed over the years to help clients who struggle with important decisions.

Decisiology has three objectives:

- To improve the outcomes of specific decisions people face.

- To help them make better decisions by themselves.

- To identify the common thread behind those decisions people find particularly challenging; and follow that thread down to its deepest roots.

INTRODUCTION

On 23 April 2016 a rather unusual production was mounted at the Royal Shakespeare Company Theatre in Stratford-upon-Avon, in the heart of the English Midlands. Some of the best Shakespearean actors in the land gathered on stage to celebrate the anniversary of the Bard's death, on St George's Day, 400 years earlier, on a date that happens to coincide with the playwright's birthday.

They were not there to perform an entire play, or even a whole scene, but instead focused on a single passage of dramatic verse, arguably the most famous line ever written for the stage. In a comedic and illuminating sketch, the likes of Dame Judi Dench, Benedict Cumberbatch, Harriet Walter, David Tennant and Sir Ian McKellen busily coached Paapa Essiedu, the RSC's Hamlet of the time, on the most perfect possible delivery of the first ten words of Hamlet's soliloquy, "To be or not to be, that is the question."

To this end, each of them recommended that the novice Hamlet should stress only one word – though, of course, they disagreed on *which* word, often with great comic effect (starting with Tim Minchin's "to be *or* not to be?").

The last performer to grace the stage was no thespian, despite being a well-known actor on the world stage: Prince Charles, first in line to the throne. Not entirely dissimilar, in this respect, to Hamlet himself. And when he delivered the famous verse, the word he chose to stress was the very last one: "That is the *question.*"

***

In London's Bloomsbury, safely hidden in the vaults of the British Museum is one of the rarest books in the world – one of only two remaining copies of the *First Quarto*, the name given to the first published version of *Hamlet*, dated 1603. The version performed nowadays is the third iteration. The *First Quarto* differs from the later versions in at least one major respect: the first lines of the "To be or not to be" soliloquy.

In this original version the words are: "To be, or not to be, I there's the point." It seems that somehow, the *question* has already been answered.

"To be or not to be" is the genesis of each and every choice we make. Something simply is or isn't. And the same applies to us. We decide to be or not to be, to live or not to live, to do or not to do.

But whereas the popular version of the soliloquy indicates that, as human beings, we are faced with a decision of a binary nature (1 or 0, Yes or No), the original text hints at a different consideration: the *point* is not the outcome (*to be* or *not to be*), but the very fact that we face a decision (to be *or* not to be). And "I", this singular word thrown in between two propositions – I, the quintessence of being human – defines what it means to stand in front of the abyss. I only truly exist when I stand there, in front of the choice I need to make, ready to decide on being or not being, doing or not doing.

The abyss illustrates what it means *not* to be human. Like a dark lake, it sends a reverse image back to us, our mirror image as humans: to be or not to be, mediated through this obscure spectrum.

In his essay *The Rebel*, the French philosopher Albert Camus describes a man who reacts to the meaningless and absurd nature of the world, trying to make sense of it and to make the right choices for himself. Camus asks: "Who is the rebel? First and foremost, he is a man who says no. But while he refuses, he doesn't renounce: he is also a man who says yes."

The opposite of a decision is not the opposite decision. It is *renouncing*: renouncing our essential ability and duty to decide. To quote the philosopher Martin Buber, "if there were a Devil, it would not be one who decided against God, but one who, in eternity, came to no decision."

Two years ago I attended a conference run by the Thomson Reuters Foundation on the theme of "Slavery in the 21st century". Its Chief Executive, Monique Villa, asserted that slavery is life without decision making. What the Foundation observed was that people who were freed from slavery had, through their captivity, lost the ability to make decisions. For this reason, setting them free is not enough: they must also be taught to decide for themselves.

Decisions have the ability to free us. However, if most of us are free in the legal sense, are our minds and our souls equally free? Are we genuinely free to make the decisions we want to make, including the choice to lead the life we want to live?

Or do we simply make the decisions that we cannot escape? Are we following compulsions set by others, a society's expectations? Are we slaves to a false sense of fate? And if it turns out that we are, how can we then break free from our shackles?

This is our challenge. And if the answer is not "self-help" (which to my mind conjures up the image of a neglected self-service motorway rest area), it is probably "Self help" (in Jungian psychology the Self, with a capital S, refers to the transcendent, permanent part of ourselves, in contrast to the ego, which evolves in the present). If we can start to tune into our true Self, we can set about living the life we were put on this Earth for.

As your *self*-appointed guide on this journey, I will take you now on a voyage of exploration. Think of it like an archaeological mission, such as the journey that Howard Carter and Lord Carnarvon made to Egypt in the early 20th century. This led to the discovery in 1922 of Tutankhamun's tomb, with its fabulous treasures, enriching our knowledge of ancient Egypt. The undertaking was achieved at the cost of much digging, much dusting, and probably much desperation before the final triumph!

As archaeologists of volition, we need to be prepared for a similarly ambitious mission. It will involve commitment and strength, as we dig for psychological archetypes and long-forgotten events and thought processes, as well as deep-rooted emotions.

Whereas Howard Carter's main tools, in the Valley of the Kings, were trowels and hand brooms, our toolkit will include reflection, philosophy, psychology and etymology.

When I started this project, reflecting on the words *decision* and *decisive,* often repeating them in my mind, I found that my brain frequently made an associative leap to *incision* and *incisive*. It occurred to me that this linkage gives us one reason for the pains we experience when making decisions.

This is confirmed by etymology. *Caedere*, the Latin root of the word "decision", literally means "to cut off". If decisions are about cutting ourselves off from other choices, other opportunities, away from the possibility of better outcomes, and in a way that limits our freedom, this goes a long way to explaining why making decisions can be so daunting.

At the same time, we can look at this from a different viewpoint. Perhaps the "cutting off" of decision making could equally refer to the freedom we gain once we have severed the shackles of indecisiveness and procrastination.

This cutting off may be what helps us summon the resolution to act, once the deliberation process is over. Making our choice and acting upon it brings deliberation to an end, as we cut ourselves away from any other options. If decisions are going to serve us, they must be performed with a positive intent in mind. Painful they may be, but rewardingly so.

Travelling still further back in time, I noticed that the ancient Greek word for "decision" has the same root as the word meaning "separation". But it also means "judgement", with a divine connotation – referring to a higher, almost metaphysical form of decision making. This is reminiscent of King Solomon's Judgement, after two mothers each claimed the same baby as their own. Calling for a sword, Solomon declared, "Divide the child in two, and give half to one, and half to the other." One mother thought the ruling fair, but the other begged Solomon, "Give the baby to her, just don't kill him!" The king identified the second woman as the true mother, since a mother would even give up her baby if this meant saving its life. In this instance, an apparently cold and cruel decision leads by stealth to true Justice.

And just what is this ancient Greek word meaning decision, separation and judgement? I found myself staring at my etymological dictionary with a sense of stunned recognition: the ancient Greek word for decision is none other than *krisis*.

If decisions are a type of crisis, our struggles to deal with them may not be so surprising after all. This may be exactly what decisions want us to experience. It follows that the best way to deal with decisions is the way we respond to other crises (or at least the way we know we should!) – that is, not by panicking, self-doubting or renouncing what is difficult or painful, but rather by listening intently to the heartbeat of a crisis, embracing it and learning from it, in order to mitigate its effects, and wherever possible turn them into opportunities.

Donning our archaeologists' hard hats we shall now begin to unearth our own decision-making processes, first exploring the land of indecision (Part I), before identifying where we may get stuck in our decisions (Part II), in order to resume the momentum (Part III) that leads us to our smartest choices (Part IV).

PART I
INDECISION, INDECISION

CHAPTER I
PARADISE LOST

Indecision, *noun.*
Lack of decision; inability to decide or tendency to change the mind frequently; hesitation or vacillation.

Webster's New World College Dictionary, 4th edition

Indecision may be the reason you are reading this book. Perhaps you feel you need some help in making choices more decisively. Or perhaps some well-meaning soul has recommended it to you.

As the above definition makes clear, indecision is the condition to which we subject ourselves when we do not want to, or cannot decide.

This is the location where I have decided to set up camp and start digging – it is exactly where the problem lies. The terrain is promising. It has been surveyed before in literature; and in real life, indeed, most of us will have found many characters whose defining trait is indecision.

The iconic example, without a doubt, is Hamlet the Dane, who cannot decide how, when or even whether to avenge his dead father, the King. This is despite having gathered all the evidence that the King died at the hands of Claudius, the King's own brother, who has since usurped the throne of Denmark to become King himself, after marrying Hamlet's mother, Gertrude.

In Dostoyevsky's *Notes from the Underground*, the isolated and unnamed anti-hero divides his life between ennui and inactivity.

However, the most extreme incarnation of indecision must be Ivan Goncharov's protagonist Oblomov, in the novel of the same name. Oblomov is a young Russian nobleman who, throughout his life, is incapable of making decisions, or engaging in any meaningful activity. As a result, he spends most of his time in his room or his bed, something he blames on a rare form of apathy he calls "oblomovitis".

What all these characters share is a pathological inability to decide, and therefore, to act.

In *Notes from the Underground*, one reason Dostoyevsky's narrator gives for his ennui is the struggle between his own competing points of view:

> "You see, gentlemen: reason is a good thing, there's no denying it, but reason is only reason and satisfies only man's rational faculty, whereas volition is a manifestation of the whole life – and by that I mean the whole of life, together with reason and the head-scratching that goes with it."

The question posed by Dostoyevsky's anti-hero is: how can we make a decision when different parts of our mind want two (or more) different things? This will perhaps strike you as a realistic scenario, in which you may well have found yourself.

ORIENTATION POINT

Indecisiveness can result when we have two desires in conflict with each other – the head/heart opposition is best known, but other binaries are also possible, such as work/play, long-term/short-term or affordability/quality. Careful weighing of true priorities, applying intuition as well as logic, is the optimum way forward.

The other reason these characters cannot decide or act is that there is something deceptively comfortable about the pre-decision state: by not deciding, I gain access to the magical world of virtual reality, where two contradictory options can happily co-exist. Since I haven't decided and haven't cut myself off from any of the options, I can live in the comforting illusion that choice will remain a possibility.

The psychoanalyst and philosopher Erich Fromm describes, in *The Feeling of Powerlessness*, a gifted writer who wanted to bring out the most important book in world literature. Despite having only a handful of ideas about what he would write, he enjoyed fantasizing about what the impact of his book would be. He let his friends believe he'd been working on the book for seven years, but in reality he had not written even a single word. "The older such people get," Fromm muses, "the more they cling to the illusion that one day they will do it."

Research by the University of Chicago and Duke University shows that we often irrationally refuse to commit to a choice, even though we know this is counterproductive. "Closing a door on an option is experienced as a loss, and people are willing to pay a price to avoid the emotion of loss," says Dan Ariely of Duke University.

It seems that when we cannot decide, either we are immobilized by the various options in front of us or we take the easy road and simply mothball them all for future consideration. And the former often leads to the latter.

However, let's dig deeper. What causes us to react like this in the first place? What is it about decisions that induces the type of *crisis* etymology points to?

We would do well to remember the Greek root of the word "decision", which means "separation"; and the Latin root, which means "cutting off". Does this only relate to our separation from alternative options, or from the state of indecision? Or is there possibly more to it than that? Could this separation also mirror a deeper and inner psychological reality?

According to the Jungian psychoanalyst James Hollis, "the primary motive, the hidden agenda in any relationship, is the yearning to return." I believe this is not limited to the relationship between two people. It also applies to our relationship with ourselves. The problem that decisions create is that they test our most essential relationship, by asking us: What do you want? Which part of you wants this? Which part of you blocks this decision? And while we are on this topic, does any of us ever know with any certainty what we want?

For Hollis, the "yearning to return" is a trauma, which is deeply engraved in our DNA as members of the human race. "All peoples, past and present, have had their mythology of a lost paradise. [...] Perhaps this tribal memory is but the neurological hologram of our own birth trauma, a separation from which we never fully recover."

We find this theme of the lost paradise played out in most fairy tales. In these stories, it isn't Eden that the protagonists are seeking to return to, but a Royal Palace (for example, in the Snow White tale) or the comfortable family home (Little Red Riding Hood) or part of that home, after being sent to live below stairs (Cinderella, Harry Potter).

In *The Uses of Enchantment*, Bruno Bettelheim explores the psychoanalytical meaning and broadly positive impact of fairy tales, those stories read to us at a time when we are at our most impressionable. He also warns us against the dangers of not fully embracing the move away from heavenly Eden.

Regression to this paradisal state, he argues, undermines our independence and our individuation – the process, according to Carl Jung, by which the self is formed through the integration of the unconscious (both personal and collective) into consciousness. To develop we need to change, and change means giving up something we had formerly enjoyed. These stories also tell us not to be afraid of moving away from dependency on other people. The transitional period to a new mode of living may be tough, but we will emerge richer and happier. "Those who are reluctant to risk such a transformation," says Bettelheim, "never gain the kingdom."

The reason why they never gain the kingdom is the same reason why later in life they cannot make decisions: they have not ascended to the new mode of living, the "higher and better plane". Let us call this plane: *consciousness*.

Whilst it is self-evident that there is no proper decision without consciousness, it is essential to realize that there is no consciousness without transformation. And this transformation comes from abandoning any intentions of returning to the lost paradise. This forms the *genesis* of our decisions, and of us as decision-makers: the incision that cuts us off from any illusory, dreamlike, magical and virtual universe, to project us into the real world.

ORIENTATION POINT

We may think a decision is just a matter of bringing about the best available outcome, but it can be more fundamental than this. One of the things that may hold us back is an attachment to known comforts, or conversely a fear of the unknown. Growing into greater maturity and consciousness is painful but rewarding, as it is the source of our best decision making.

Expressions like "yearning to return" and "lost paradise" are reminiscent of the experience of peoples who have fled their countries, whether in biblical or more recent times. The word *diaspora* (from the ancient Greek for "scattered across") relates to their collective experience. At a psychological level, I believe that diaspora is an effective metaphor for a psyche that is scattered across, dis-integrated, and can either yearn for an illusory "return" or for a healthy re-connection and individuation. This is the real fork in the road: not necessarily the struggle to choose between two options on any given day but, more meaningfully, the decision to either return to a fictitious paradise and false sense of security, or to take the higher road toward affirmation, reality and wholeness.

In this context, those who find themselves unable to "make the cut" are likely to have built a variety of effective defence mechanisms to avoid making decisions. This is what we explore in the next chapter.

CHAPTER 2
DEFENCE FORCES

Mono-living

A London newspaper recently featured an article about a trend called "Mono-living". According to its author, choice is overrated. One of the advocates of the trend is Mark Zuckerberg, the Facebook CEO and co-founder. Apparently, Zuckerberg sticks to one simple outfit of which he owns many copies: grey T-shirt and grey hoodie. "I really want to clear my life," he once said, "so that I have to make as few decisions as possible about anything except how to best serve this community. I feel like I'm not doing my job if I spend any of my energy on things that are silly or frivolous."

I don't intend to offer a critique of Zuckerberg's sartorial taste. I have a different point to make, which is that many of us have become adepts of mono-living, not necessarily in our choice of clothes (or other similarly trivial issues) but, more broadly, in our approach to important decisions. Why decide on something new when the status quo seems much more efficient?

This is how we risk becoming creatures of habit and may end up getting stuck. It is also, however, an effective defence mechanism, creating the illusion that we are more focused and efficient. Yet more focus on being stale isn't particularly desirable! And I'm sure the Facebook CEO shows more interest in his business decisions than in his wardrobe selection.

ORIENTATION POINT

Following our tried-and-tested methods may seem like a worthwhile point of focus for our efforts. It may even bring us to some important decisions. But perhaps it's more important to question whether those tried-and-tested methods are truly adequate. Could it be that they are holding us back?

What about our other defence mechanisms?

Outsourcing

Another important refuge we seek when avoiding decisions is our reliance on – and misplaced hope in – fate. Our Roman ancestors read the future in birds' entrails. Our belief in fate is perhaps scarcely less superstitious.

Closer to our time, in his 1971 cult classic novel *The Dice Man*, George Cockcroft, writing as Luke Rhinehart, tells of a disillusioned psychiatrist who starts making decisions based on the roll of a die. Each time, fate selects one of six options.

This story is partly autobiographical. The young Cockcroft, at the time a shy student of and lecturer in psychology, had the idea that by rolling dice to make decisions he could add more variety and risk to his life, expand his horizons and enrich his personality. Instructing a class in the ideas of Nietzsche and Sartre as part of a seminar on freedom, he offered the view that the ultimate freedom might be to escape both habit and causality and make all one's decisions on the roll of dice. The students reacted so positively to this suggestion that it gave Cockcroft the idea to write his bestselling novel.

Thirty years after the publication of *The Dice Man*, the London journalist Tim Adams travelled to the United States to track Cockcroft down and interview him. He concludes his article with these words: "So does he still believe that by dicing, anybody can still be anybody? […] "Well, no," he says, and laughs. "But anybody can still be a lot more people than they think, but then I guess that doesn't make quite such a good proverb."

This quote illustrates that by outsourcing our decisions to fate, we do not expand the person we are; instead, we split ourselves into different personas. And this, in turn, takes us in the opposite direction to the path we should pursue, which is the path toward individuation and self-fulfilment.

Another version of Luke Rhinehart's dice is the *Magic 8-Ball*. This was developed in the 1950s and manufactured by Mattel. You pose a question to the plastic ball, then turn it over to reveal a written answer. Today the slogan reads: "It makes decisions for you! It offers 20 potential outcomes, of which 10 are positive, and the rest are either neutral or negative." Responses include: "Without a doubt", "Most likely", "Ask again later" and "Don't count on it". This personal voice humanizes fate, turning it into helpful guidance, in contrast to the impersonal cast of a die.

Admittedly, I don't know anybody who uses dice or Magic 8-Balls to help them make important decisions. However, many of us are regular readers of the horoscope section in the daily newspapers; and just as many will also use the concept of fate to wriggle out of responsibility for unwanted outcomes.

ORIENTATION POINT

Decision making often takes place amidst uncertainties: we take action having evaluated *possible* consequences but without knowing whether the desired outcomes will follow. The simple way to describe this approach is "risk". When risks don't play out as hoped, the problem with blaming fate is that we may start to feel victimized by outside forces working against us. A healthier attitude is to make positive contingency plans to prepare for worst-case scenarios. Some risks will work in our favour; others, inevitably, will not.

There is another variation on this theme of outsourcing our responsibility toward our own decisions. "Why don't you decide? It's all the same to me." Delegating the decision to someone else in this way may not be a matter of consciously deferring to their greater wisdom: instead, it may simply be a form of surrender.

Moreover, when the other party is equally indecisive, this can lead to a comical bout of ping pong until exhaustion takes hold, and a decision is finally made by default!

If the other person has our best interests at heart, we may end up with a favourable outcome. However, even if this happens, our self-belief, our sense of ourselves as effective agents of our own development, is hardly reinforced by this kind of proxy decision making.

Procrastination

The next defence strategy is the endless postponement of decisions: procrastination. Occasionally, it will be in our best interest not to decide immediately, and instead give ourselves time for reflection. The underlying idea is that a more informed decision is likely to be a better one. However, it is clear that some of us exploit this principle as a pretext for avoiding decisions, hoping that if we wait long enough, the choice will be made for us.

My main issue with this approach is that it relies on a false premise: that we can control the timing of our decisions. Pushing things into the future creates the illusion that we have mastery over our decision making, whereas in reality postponing a decision is often akin to negating it. Although we think we are exercising our power, we are, in fact, relinquishing it.

ORIENTATION POINT

Even when it seems mature and wise to postpone a decision, we should question whether this is really the case. Sometimes people invoke good strategy as a disguise for trepidation.

It is good to bear in mind that the decision I refuse to take today and postpone until tomorrow will be necessarily a different decision. The variables around it will have changed, not just the timing. In some cases, a previously available option may have disappeared – and even if it hasn't, the conditions of its availability will have evolved.

As the Greek philosopher Heraclitus observed: "We cannot step twice into the same stream, for the second time the stream has flowed onward, and we have flowed onward as well."

The unspoken motto of procrastination should be: "The decision is dead, long live the decision!" In other words, let us not delude ourselves into thinking we are dealing with the same decision: we are either dealing with a new decision or with the ghost of a defunct one.

Of course, procrastination can find its roots in laziness. In his *Treatise on the Origin of Languages*, the 18th-century French philosopher Jean-Jacques Rousseau expressed the view that indolence is deeply ingrained in a person's character. He wrote that "the extent of man's natural laziness is inconceivable […]. If we paid close attention to it, we would realize that we only work so that we can rest; it is laziness that makes us hard-working."

However, procrastination – like the broader quality of indecision – can have other sources. One of them is the pursuit of perfection.

Perfectionism

Perfectionism is often used as a variant of procrastination, an excuse to keep postponing our decisions and actions. In a whole range of situations many people will feel it is laudable to aim for optimum results, leaving no room for imperfection. On the other hand, there will be occasions when spending more money or effort to improve a good outcome even more is not the best use of one's time.

One of my clients who runs a luxury hotel group was recently celebrating the news that his own hotel had reached an unprecedented level in its quality standards, with a score of 92 per cent. I think I may have upset him when I mischievously asked what was wrong with the remaining 8 per cent. He answered: "In this business, if you aim for 100 per cent, you quickly go bankrupt!" His point was that you end up spending vast amounts on luxuries that no customer will even notice, let alone appreciate.

The same is true of much of our decision making: aiming for 100 per cent runs the risk of your bankrupting yourself psychologically. In any case, if we seek to make decisions only when we are in control of the outcome, we end up never deciding on anything.

As part of this quest for perfection, we will often blame a lack of knowledge: "I can't decide until I have all the information in hand." Secretly, deep down, we know that this is another form of procrastination, and we will never really have all the knowledge we wish for. The film maker Abbas Kiarostami, the only Iranian who won the Palme d'Or at the Cannes Film Festival, said in 2013: "In my films I try to give people as little information as possible, which is still much more than what they get in real life. I feel that they should be grateful for the little bit of information I give them." In a similar way, when making decisions, we should be grateful for the information we have, rather than fearful about the knowledge we lack.

This points to one of the greatest myths around procrastination: the idea that if I postpone today's decision until tomorrow, I will be better informed then than I am now. If we are inclined this way, we need to ask ourselves, what is this critical information that will make all the difference? In other words – as much as I am disinclined to publicize my age – what will I learn between today and tomorrow that will make the 17,521-day-old version of me better able to decide than the 17,520-day old individual I am now? The answer is likely to be: not much!

However, if such reflections point us in the direction of any critical information that we may be lacking, we should then employ all our energies to finding it ... today!

ORIENTATION POINT

The lack of relevant information is often used as a handy excuse for delaying decision making. If you believe you need more information, switch to research mode, without delay. But don't *over*-research – another way we can fool ourselves to remain undecided.

The quest for perfection does not merely show lack of realism: it can also be regarded as narcissistic. Imperfection is intrinsic to human nature, yet many of the goals we set up for ourselves ignore this fact. When idealism infects our decision making, we can start entertaining dangerously unrealistic ideas about our own capabilities.

We are reminded by the ancient Kabbalists that the first letter of the first word of the first book of the Bible is *Beth*. However, in the Hebrew alphabet this is not the first but the second letter. The first letter, *Aleph*, is reserved for God, for what is absolute and perfect.

The Kabbalists also noted that the shape of the letter *Beth* – ב – starts from the right with a small "tail", which seems to link it up – albeit tenuously – to the invisible, the immaterial, the eternal. This letter, the first of the book of books, reminds us of the true nature of our relationship with perfection: fundamentally remote and fragile.

When it comes to decision making, the impossible quest for perfection gives us the perfect alibi to keep living in the virtual world – where perfection is always a possibility. The problem is that whilst we entertain this illusion, we do not live. This idea is reminiscent of Anna Freud's prosaic yet insightful line: "In our dreams, we have our eggs cooked exactly how we want, but we can't eat them."

Perhaps we should go as far as *celebrating* imperfection. This is the approach used by researcher Brené Brown in her book *The Gifts of Imperfection*. In her words: "Perfectionism is not the path that leads us to our gifts and to our sense of purpose; it's the hazardous detour." She explains that perfectionism is destructive, because there is no such thing as perfection. "It is a kind of Sisyphean quest, which can only lead us to failure, the one thing perfectionism dreads!" This recalls words by another author, Anne Wilson Schaef, for whom perfectionism is "self-abuse of the highest order".

Osmosis

The ultimate defence mechanism to justify indecisiveness is the process by which *not deciding* becomes who we are. This behaviour protects us because, as it infiltrates our character, we are unlikely to be solicited for decisions by others, let alone make them ourselves. As we lose faith in our opinions, this psychological device ends up determining our character, through a vicious circle of self-doubt.

Of course, a psychological condition may be the source rather than the consequence of an inability to decide: in neurology, *aboulia* (from the Greek, meaning "absence of will") is one of the recognized Diminished Motivation Disorders. Patients with aboulia are unable to act or make decisions independently.

At the other extreme, psychological disorders can lead to sufferers having no difficulty in making decisions, though their choices are of a self-harming nature.

We have briefly entered the realm of psychological and neurological conditions, beyond the scope of this book. However, for the vast majority of us, the difficulties we face in our decision making can be healed through the method that underlies much of this book: self-reflection.

The opposite of neurosis is a process which the neo-Freudian psychoanalyst Karen Horney called "self-realization". Horney compared this process to an acorn that grows into a tree. "Similarly, the human individual, given a chance, tends to develop his particular human potentialities. He will develop then the unique alive forces of his real self: the clarity and depth of his own feelings, thoughts, wishes, interests; the ability to tap his own resources, the strength of his will power." At the same time, the path towards self-realization offers an escape from one's own deep-rooted anxieties.

In our present journey, if we want to defeat the type of anxiety that decisions bring about, what the tree symbolizes is the higher level of consciousness we should aspire to grow into. Achieving this level of consciousness about our decisions requires us to step over or knock through the defence mechanisms we have built for ourselves over the years, to discover what lies on the other side – the aspects of ourselves that our defences have been hiding all along.

CHAPTER 3
PROJECT FEAR

"Worrying is like paying a debt you don't owe."

Mark Twain

In 1929, to protect their country from another German invasion, the French government started the construction of an impressive line of concrete fortifications along its eastern border with Germany, Luxembourg and Switzerland. The Maginot Line was a huge military engineering structure. Its construction ended in 1940. The northern end of the Maginot Line stopped at the border with Belgium. Ironically, 1940 was also the year Germany invaded France ... through Belgium.

Defence mechanisms can be very complex. However, complexity does not imply necessarily that they are effective. The psychological defences described in the previous chapter are complex too; but they can fail in their mission, allowing the enemy, the hostile force they were made to fend off, to invade their territory.

What is this hostile force that our defence mechanisms are trying to protect us from? I am conscious that this chapter's title rather gives the game away!

Fear is not always a negative emotion. It can make us more alert to unforeseen risks, and it can help us to protect others as well as ourselves against potential dangers.

Franklin D Roosevelt famously said in his 1933 inaugural speech as US President that there is nothing to fear, not even fear itself. As we all know, fear can easily take over, inhibiting us and stifling our ambitions and growth. So the picture is not black and white: fear can be a positive or a negative force, and it is probably both at the same time.

This paradox is possible because we are animated by two different goals: a prevention focus (we want to protect ourselves) and a promotion focus (we want to make progress).

In 2010, two years after the start of the global recession, a team of professors from Harvard Business School embarked on a year-long research project to identify those companies that could best survive the crisis and discover what was their common denominator. They studied almost 5,000 corporations and analysed their strategy and corporate performance during the previous three global recessions: the 1980 crisis (to 1982), the 1990 slowdown (to 1991) and the 2000 bust (to 2002).

The first important finding was that only a small number of companies – approximately 9 per cent of the sample – were doing better three years after a recession than they had before it, outperforming their peers by 10 per cent or more in terms of sales and profit growth. The vast majority of companies had either disappeared (17 per cent had gone bankrupt or been taken over) or hadn't recovered their pre-recession growth rate (80 per cent of the surviving companies), and for half of those, they hadn't even recovered their pre-recession sales and profit levels.

The Harvard researchers also found that companies could be assigned to one of these four categories:

- *Prevention-focused companies*, dedicated to avoiding losses and cutting risks. Compared with their rivals, they developed a more defensive strategy.

- *Promotion-focused companies,* continuing to invest in their future growth through a more offensive strategy.

- *Pragmatic companies,* adopting a dual approach of defensive and offensive moves.

- *Progressive companies*, a sub-section of pragmatic companies: what sets them apart is their efforts to strike an optimal balance between offensive and defensive moves.

The last category is best positioned for success. Companies within this group were judged to have the highest probability – 37 per cent – of breaking away from the pack. "These companies reduce costs selectively by focusing more on operational efficiency than their rivals do, even as they invest relatively comprehensively in the future by spending on marketing, R&D, and new assets. Their multipronged strategy […] is the best antidote to a recession."

If we apply these powerful findings to ourselves, how can we best manage our chances of success? The answer is: similarly, by finding the optimal balance between the impulses toward prevention and promotion. This implies accounting for, but not being overridden by, our fears.

If "conquering fear", as Bertrand Russell once wrote, "is the beginning of wisdom", then a good place from which to lead the charge is an understanding of fear and its variant manifestations, in the context of decision making.

La peur n'évite pas le danger. This popular French expression, which translates as "fear does not prevent danger", draws an important distinction: these are not two sides of the same coin. Fear is merely a vision of the mind. It is not a stimulus, something we receive from the outside world (from that source we receive *threats*, not fear), but something we *project* onto those threats. In the words attributed to Winston Churchill: "Fear is a reaction, courage is a decision."

The title of this chapter is an allusion to the UK's EU referendum of June 2016, during which the "Leave" camp (committed to the UK leaving the European Union) coined the expression "Project Fear" to characterize the strategy of the "Remain" side, who were accused of scaring people into staying in the Union. However, it is clear that both sides of the "Brexit" debate used the fear factor to persuade people to follow a particular direction. This shows that fear is not only a decision-inhibitor but can also be a decision-shaper, something that influences us beyond reason.

It is time now to glance at an argument in classical economics: expected utility theory. "The expected utility of an act," we are told, "is a weighted average of the *utilities* of each of its possible outcomes. The *utility* of an outcome measures the extent to which that outcome is preferred, or preferable, to the alternatives."

In their seminal work *Decision Making under Risk*, published in 1979, Daniel Kahneman and Amos Tversky challenged the classic view of expected utility theory as the most accurate model to describe how we make decisions. They introduced a new behavioural dimension to their theory of decision making. Prospect theory indicates that people are loss-averse: when people are dealing with gains, they will choose the sure gain over the riskier prospect. For example, most people would prefer winning $100 with certainty to tossing a coin and taking the risk of winning either $200 or nothing. However, when faced with the options of a certain $100 loss versus a 50 per cent chance of either losing $200 or nothing, they often choose the second option. In short, the same person who is risk-seeking when faced with possible loss will be reluctant to take risks when faced with possible gain.

What prospect theory establishes therefore is that the fear of a loss drives us toward riskier behaviours in a way that cannot be explained by reason alone. Since most studies suggest that losses are twice as powerful, psychologically, as gains, we can understand why fear is such a powerful agent of irrationality in our decision making.

If we want to gain control over fear, we need to dig deeper. What is fear exactly? What is it made of?

I have come to the conclusion that decision-fear falls into seven categories, which can be grouped under two headings: *fears about the choices we make* and *fears about the consequences of our choices*.

Fears about the choices we make

1 Fear of rejecting a better option

The fear of rejecting a better option makes many people feel paralysed when it comes to committing to a decision. And despite the advice from self-help literature on procrastination (the plus/minus lists and other "one-stop" techniques), this remains a challenging issue for many.

A few years ago, I decided to take a trip to Cuba with the dual purpose of meeting local artists and realizing my long-held dream of photographing Havana. My two objectives soon merged into one, as I was keen to see the island and its capital city not as a mere tourist but through the eyes of those artists I was intent on meeting. Many of my photographs ended up being of artists, their workshops or their art. It so happened that after visiting a collective of print artists, I took one of my favourite shots inside a nearby derelict residential block. Someone – probably one of the collective's artists – had covered the entire wall in the entrance area with two horizontal halves of bright white and vivid green paint, upon which he painted the words: *No te preocupes por lo que tengo, preocupate por lo que te falta*, which translates as: "Do not concern yourself with what I have, think instead about what you are lacking." I felt that these words resonated strongly in a city like Havana, a notoriously destitute place, where this message takes on particular profundity. This is also a thought on which many of us in the West could usefully meditate.

The antithesis to this message is summarized by our 21st-century acronym FOMO, or Fear of Missing Out. To return for a few seconds to this entrance hall in Havana, FOMO is what we subject ourselves to when we are more concerned about what other people may have than what we are lacking. In the spirit of FOMO we ignore our true needs, instead focusing our attention unduly on others.

Ultimately the fear of missing out, or in the realm of decision making the fear of rejecting a better option, often gets conjoined with another fear: that of having regrets. I think most people can cope with missing out on something. What they find much harder is dealing with the associated regret of not following the other, better route. However, as we discussed earlier, decisions have a built-in expiry process. After a decision is taken, it isn't a decision any more, it has become either an act or a non-act. And what is left of the decision itself is a mere memory, the ghost of the decision.

ORIENTATION POINT

Regret never serves us well, even when we make questionable decisions. Even worse is *fear* of regret, since that paralyses us into inaction. It is unhelpful, as well as philosophically invalid, to treat a rejected decision as having a life of its own, taunting us with a vision of a hypothetical alternative to the route we have in reality taken.

To use another analogy, our decisions are like butterflies. Some are dazzling and colourful, some are quite dull – but what they all have in common is that before they grow into these creatures, they pass through different development stages, first from the caterpillar (a fully autonomous being, rather like our thoughts before a decision) to the pupa, from which they will eventually emerge. The chrysalis is all that is left once the butterfly has flown away. And the butterfly never goes back to the comfort of the chrysalis. It knows that this shallow envelope has become not only too small for it, but also entirely pointless.

The chrysalis of decision making is forever irrelevant once a decision is made. There is no point in mulling over the decision itself, because nothing can change it now. It has vacated the world. It has evaporated forever. We cannot change a decision: we can only take a new one that may or may not alter its outcome.

Looking back at a situation in which we feel we have missed out can be constructive only if our sole purpose is to learn from it, rather than be remorseful. In this case, looking back will lead not to regret but to enrichment. It will inform us on *how* we made that decision, and *how* we can apply in our future development the experiences we gained. This doesn't mean that there's no room for disappointment. However, disappointment is factual, a moment of perception; whereas regret and remorse are self-consuming. (The etymology of "regret" is "to weep again", while "remorse" initially meant "to bite back". Hence the sense of an enduring pain, emotional [regret] or physical [remorse].)

Another analogy may be useful at this point. If you are unfortunate enough to find yourself chased by a wild beast, the fear of the beast catching up with you is entirely legitimate and may even help you to run faster; whereas the fear of the aftermath is simply pointless and will only feed your anxiety. Similarly, before and after a decision is made, fearing or feeling regret will not pre-empt suffering – it will only end up feeding it. The indecision related to this fear of regret does not postpone the possibility of suffering: it makes it an everyday reality.

As the psychoanalyst Marie-Louise von Franz wrote, "One needs not to be the fool who believes in nothing but happiness and then falls from the clouds, but if one always retreats at the beginning in anticipation of the suffering, that is a typical pathological reaction. It is something many neurotic people do. They try to train themselves not to suffer by always anticipating suffering. But that is typically morbid and completely prevents you from living."

On this note, let us remember that *The Time Machine* ends without the time traveller, its main protagonist. He has vanished, without even being given a name. His attraction to the unlived life has rendered him anonymous. It is revealing that at one stage, in 14th-century French, the word *regret* meant "to lament someone's death". Somehow, whenever we feel regret, we grieve for the demise of the time traveller in ourselves.

It is worth noting that our own deciding mind does not handle all types of regrets in the same manner. It differentiates between these two experiences:

- *Regret for the things we did do and wish we hadn't*
  These are known in psychology as "errors of commission". This could apply, for example, to the feelings we have after treating someone unfairly.

- *Regret for the things we did not do and we wish we had*
  These are known as "errors of omission". An example would be not having seized an opportunity that was once offered to us.

Research by Thomas Gilovich and Victoria Husted Medvec of Cornell University and Serena Chen of New York University concludes that, in the short term, regrets for commission – the things we did – affect us more than regrets for omission. However, over time, the exact opposite happens, and we end up regretting our errors of omission more than our errors of commission.

Therefore, when we reject an attractive option by choosing the status quo in preference to change, we may think we are making the conservative choice. Because we did *not* act, we run a lesser risk of regretting our decision. What research shows is that the opposite happens, as it is precisely these moments of negative/passive choice that create the most enduring feelings of regret.

The fear of regrets is one version of the fear of rejecting a better option. All this will often belong in the category that may be described as a "first world problem" (such as, where should I go on holiday?). This happens when we need to choose between two (or more) options of equal appeal.

However, there is often an added complication when the different options are not only mutually exclusive but also conducive to two potentially very different outcomes for us. Here the fear is not just of missing out on a better option, but of facing a loss versus a gain, demotion versus promotion, defeat versus victory, with potentially life-changing consequences. We come face to face with the fear of choosing the wrong option, in its most blatant manifestation.

2 Fear of choosing the wrong option

Last night, on a flight to Rome, I had a conversation with my neighbour (a private equity investor), who said to me: "I get irritated when my colleagues want to justify an investment decision based on a financial model. Ultimately, our important decisions need to rely on gut feeling, not just on Excel spreadsheets." What he was articulating was a key principle of heuristics (practical techniques for problem solving): the fact that we make many decisions, including critical ones, using the rule of thumb, not just logic. In some cases, logic is supplemented by intuition; in other instances, it is distorted by our built-in biases. With the advent of behavioural economics in the late 20th and early 21st centuries, cognitive psychologists opened a Pandora's box of those biases that take our decision making beyond the realm of rationality.

We have looked at Kahneman and Tversky's research on making decisions under risk, and the loss aversion bias. Related biases include:

- *Non-linear probability weighting*
  Decision-makers overweight small probabilities and underweight large probabilities. This reminds me of a comment made by the famed CNN travel reporter Wolf Blitzer at a recent industry conference. He told us that a large proportion of the US population was putting off travelling abroad out of fear of a terrorist attack. Yet statistics show that the risk of dying at home of electrocution is considerably higher. It turns out that foreign travel might in some circumstances be seen as the safe option, and staying home as the risky one!

- *Reference dependence*
  We tend to evaluate outcomes relative to our own arbitrary reference point (generally the status quo) and classify them as "gains" if better than the reference point, and as "losses" if worse than the reference point. For example, if you find a dollar coin in the street, you will happily pick it up – not because of the impact it has on your overall wealth (the only truly rational reference point) but because compared to the other available reference ($0 if I don't pick it up versus $1 if I do), it is likely to give satisfaction beyond what reason alone could justify.

- *Gain and loss satiation*
  As our gains and losses relative to the reference point increase in absolute value, the marginal effect on us tends to fall. This is why, if you win the lottery tonight, a $2m gain would not make you twice as happy as a $1m gain, but only marginally more so. However, this phenomenon is asymmetrical: losing $10 produces more pain than winning $10 produces pleasure.

The list of such cognitive biases is getting longer every year, as psychologists make new advances and realize how unfit our minds are at making purely rational decisions. There is even a "Cognitive Bias Codex" available online, which presents these findings in a creative and graphic way. In typical scientific style, the names of the biases keep becoming more exotic and intriguing.

Some of my all-time favourites include:

- *The Dunning-Kruger effect*, or the tendency for unskilled individuals to overestimate their own ability, as well as the tendency for experts to underestimate their own ability.

- *The curse of knowledge*, which explains why better-informed people find it extremely difficult to think about problems from the perspective of lesser-informed people.

- *The cheerleader bias*, which makes people think that individuals are more attractive when seen in a group.

- *The Von Restorff effect*, which states that an item that sticks out is more likely to be remembered than other items.

- *The Zeigarnik effect*, according to which uncompleted or interrupted tasks are remembered better than completed ones.

The awareness of our hundreds of potential biases doesn't exactly help us gain faith in our decision-making abilities. However, it does shed light on the need to double-check the motivating factors at work when we make our choices.

ORIENTATION POINT

If we think we are being impartial when we make a decision, we are wrong! All kinds of biases affect our judgement, altering our view of the relevant factors, and influencing the weight we attach to them. There is nothing wrong with this – human decision-makers have lives, unlike computer algorithms. But a degree of self-knowledge will help to ensure that our biases are less likely to become pitfalls.

At this point, we could argue that awareness of our irrationality makes our aversion to choosing the wrong option a highly rational fear! But the fear of choosing the wrong option doesn't always stem from such psychological biases. In some cases, it will come from the deadlock we face when considering one option in relation to another, when they weigh equally in our minds: we may sometimes want two things that are contradictory and mutually exclusive.

Think of the decision to buy a home. For some people this has proven to be the best investment of their lives, providing them and their families with long-term financial peace of mind; for others it has led to negative equity and the loss of decades of savings. The main differences between these two scenarios are often external changes beyond anyone's control (interest rate movements, market slumps or rises, and the like), as well as changes in personal circumstances. But how does one make this important decision, when the desire for long-term security (represented by home ownership) is at loggerheads with the equally valid need for short-term financial safety (avoiding a burdensome mortgage)?

Ultimately, every decision is about resolving a deep contradiction. In the words of author and psychiatrist Irvin Yalom: "For every 'yes' there must be a 'no'. Decisions are expensive because they demand renunciation. This phenomenon has attracted great minds throughout the ages. Aristotle imagined a hungry dog unable to choose between two equally attractive portions of food, and the medieval scholastics wrote of Buridan's ass, which starved to death between two equally sweet-smelling bales of hay."

I will happily admit that I spent most of my adult life believing that Buridan's only claim to fame was his ownership of that doomed donkey, and assuming that he was a character in some folk tale, the fictional butt of a popular joke, rather than a real living person.

On the contrary, Jean Buridan was one of the most influential French philosophers and logicians of the 14th century, and one of the greatest Aristotelians of his time. The little scenario described above is a satire against him, and his writings on moral determinism.

In 1340 Buridan, who probably never owned the indecisive donkey, wrote that "should two courses be judged equal, then the will cannot break the deadlock, all it can do is to suspend judgement until the circumstances change, and the right course of action is clear."

This view will be challenged more than three centuries later in Amsterdam by Baruch Spinoza, who argued that a man who cannot choose between two seemingly equal options cannot be regarded as fully rational:

"... if man does not act from free will, what will happen if the incentives to action are equally balanced, as in the case of Buridan's ass? [...] I am quite ready to admit, that a man placed in the equilibrium described (namely, as perceiving nothing but hunger and thirst, a certain food and a certain drink, each equally distant from him) would die of hunger and thirst. If I am asked, whether such a one should not rather be considered an ass than a man; I answer, that I do not know, neither do I know how a man should be considered, who hangs himself, or how we should consider children, fools, madmen, and so on."

The fact that this debate has engaged some of our greatest philosophers over the centuries is testimony to the significance of the issue it addresses. In modern times, we find many illustrations in the tough choices that history has imposed on men and women, especially in wartime. I recently saw a moving play at London's St James's Theatre. It was written and performed by Mona Golabek, the daughter of Viennese-born Jewish pianist Lisa Jura. Set in Vienna in 1938 and London during the war, *The Pianist of Willesden Lane* tells Lisa's true story. Her parents had two daughters but could only save one of them from the Nazi regime, as they could only obtain one ticket for the *Kindertransport*. How does a parent make such a soul-destroying choice, that will save one child but send the other in all likelihood to a premature death?

Here the question is not, "Which choice is right or wrong?", but whether having to choose in the first place is wrong. In the context of this dramatic play, refusing choice, however immoral that choice may be, would have been akin to favouring death, the "impossibility of future possibility", as Martin Heidegger put it, including the possibility of bearing witness to history. In this context, renouncing choice seems the worst option, despite the terrible alternative. Since we find ourselves in the domain of the arts, I'm minded now to turn to painting.

"What I am attempting in each picture is nothing other than this: to bring together in a living and viable way the most different and the most contradictory elements in the greatest possible freedom."

These are the words of the highly respected German painter Gerhard Richter. What Richter implies is that it is naïve to expect decisions to bring closure. Decisions are merely about creating the least imperfect and most viable balance between conflicting views. And they are about achieving balance with the greatest freedom from pre-conceived or pre-programmed notions in our minds.

If this is about freedom, it is also necessarily about movement. When facing the fear of making a wrong decision, it should give us some relief to realize that a decision that is viewed today as wrong may deliver unexpected positive benefits tomorrow, possibly more so than the seemingly right option today. The wrong option today may well turn out to be the right option in the end.

This argument was given an interesting spin by the economist John Kay in his book *Obliquity*. Kay's idea is that many goals are more likely to be achieved when pursued indirectly. He points out that "the richest men and women are not the most materialistic"; the same way, "the happiest people are not necessarily those who focus on happiness, and the most profitable companies are not always the most profit-oriented, as the recent financial crisis showed us."

On this note, we all remember the words delivered by John F Kennedy at Rice University Stadium, Houston, Texas, in September 1962: "We choose to go to the Moon in this decade and do the other things not because they are easy, but because they are hard; because that goal will serve to organize and measure the best of our energies and skills." This is the rhetoric Kennedy used to convince the American taxpayer to part with $5.4bn in order to fund his endeavour. From Kennedy's point of view, this was not a $5.4bn second-class return ticket to the moon, but a first-class investment in the nation's character, the anticipated yet oblique side-effect of the *Apollo 11* mission.

ORIENTATION POINT

The best decision making is not necessarily the most direct: it depends on the nature of your goals. Some desirable values are by-products, which emerge unbidden – the obvious examples being love, success and happiness. People who strive too consciously, too directly, for such objectives are more likely to find them elusive.

Fears about the consequences of our choices

1 Fear of failure

Often we may feel confident that our choice is right – in which case there is little or no fear of making the wrong decision or missing out on a better future. However, fear of another nature sets in: that of failing to turn opportunity into success. Being well qualified and prepared is not quite enough: in addition, it is good to be aware of the many factors that may affect our chances of success – some external (for example, unexpected changes in the environment, in other people's attitudes and so on), some internal (such as self-doubt, or a re-evaluation of priorities).

The 1st-century Stoic philosopher Epictetus begins his manual, the *Enchiridion*, with an important distinction:

> "Of things some are in our power, and others are not. In our power are opinion, movement toward a thing, desire, aversion (turning from a thing); and in a word, whatever are our acts: not in our power are the body, property, reputation, offices (magisterial power), and in a word, whatever are not our acts."

Epictetus goes on to explain that if we try to control those things that are not within our control, we will make ourselves miserable. Fulfilment comes from seeking to act only upon those things that can be influenced by our actions, and even these are few and far between.

> "If then you attempt to avoid only the things contrary to nature which are within your power, you will not be involved in any of the things which you would avoid. But if you attempt to avoid disease or death or poverty, you will be unhappy. Take away the aversion from all things which are not in your power."

This is followed in a typically Stoic way by these words:

> "But, for the present, totally suppress desire: for, if you desire any of the things which are not in your own control, you must necessarily be disappointed."

Epictetus does not argue for banishing desire outright, but he warns us against *unbridled* desire, our tendency to get carried away striving for the unobtainable.

Now, it seems clear that failure is one of those things, like reputation or health, that is – at least partially – outside our control. We may live under the illusion that we can control our level of success or failure, but we do so at our peril. In fact, if we were able to control the outcome of a decision, there would be no need to decide in the first place!

We are bound to accept that engaging in decision making involves the acceptance of risk as a key part of the equation. We can try to mitigate risk through our actions on the things we control – for example, to a certain extent, our knowledge and our preparation. However, we will only bring frustration on ourselves if we try to gain control over anything that sits outside our sphere of influence.

If risk is embedded in every single decision we make, it follows logically that fear of failure isn't fear of risk (since risk is a "given"), but rather fear of the *consequences* of risk (of which loss is one among many), and the uncertainty surrounding those consequences.

The Greeks coined the perfect word for the unexpected consequences of risk: *chaos*. Today we interpret chaos as a synonym for total confusion and disorder. The etymology of the word points us in another direction: *Chaos* originally meant a gaping void, which is vast and empty; in other words, an abyss.

This is reminiscent of the abyss we encountered at the start of our journey – the abyss that every decision opens, projecting our own image back at ourselves. As I suggested there, we are only truly alive, as human beings, when we accept to stand at the edge of the abyss, ready to face our decisions.

Since our mission is exploratory and – at least metaphorically – archaeological, we need to be prepared to use our ropes, harnesses and other tackle to abseil down into the gaping void that is chaos.

Almost 3,000 years ago, Hesiod described in his *Theogony* the genealogy of the Greek gods and the formation of the world. In this account the gods arise from the Void (or Chaos), Earth and Eros. Different sources in antiquity have their own different take on how these ancient Gods originated – not a surprising revelation for anyone who has tried and failed to create their own family tree! Whereas Hesiod (c700 BC) saw Eros as born out of Chaos, Parmenides (c400 BC) regards him as first of all the gods to come into existence. According to Aristophanes (c400 BC), Eros "mated in the deep Abyss with dark Chaos, winged like himself, and thus hatched forth our race, which was the first to see the light."

ORIENTATION POINT

The fundamental importance of desire to the human condition is reflected in the part Eros (desire) played in the creation of the gods, according to ancient Greek sources. To repress our desires is unhelpful. Any creation – and therefore any decision – requires the encounter between Eros and Chaos. The resulting outcome when desire touches chaos is that both are turned into a new combined reality.

Whatever the precise genealogy, what remains constant throughout antiquity is the fundamental and essential connection between Chaos and Eros, or in other words, between Abyss and Desire. Eros does not solely mean desire of a physical nature: it is much closer to what Heraclitus called *Physis*, the force present in all living things, the source of our energy and creativity. (A similar concept, by the way, can be found in the Indian *Shakti*, the primal energy of *Kundalini* and the Chinese concept of *Chi*).

Reflecting on these matters, we can see that Chaos is not the opposite of creation but its source (if Eros is born of Chaos) or its necessary partner. Either way, Chaos cannot achieve creation without Eros. If Chaos is the Abyss, Eros is the sky. As James Hollis has rightly noted, the word *desire* itself has its root in the Latin *de-sidere*, meaning "of the stars".

It follows that chaos, and the fear thereof (the fear of the consequences of a failed action), should not hinder us, as any creative or meaningful decision will need to tap into the energies of both chaos and desire.

The only other option is to remain stuck on the vast plain of indecision, staring at the gaping void between the Abyss and the Sky, between Chaos and Eros. This is what happens when we merely contemplate their infinite separation, rather than facilitate their necessary encounter.

The duality between Chaos and Eros may remind us of the binary dilemma we face in our decisions: *it will necessarily be a choice between right and wrong,* says our inner voice. Yet the Greek myths imply the notion that such a binary vision of the world is a false construct. To superimpose this construct on our decisions is to entrap ourselves in the repetition-compulsion of our inability to decide. The more we see the world as binary, the more we get stuck midway between Chaos and Eros; the more we try to distinguish right from wrong, the less we are able to discern between them. Our problem comes from the fact that we often superimpose a false moral construct ("right" vs "wrong") onto decisions that are not between a moral and an immoral or even a less moral choice. For example, if I choose this job versus that one, will it be the "right" or the "wrong" choice? Reducing our decisions to such alternatives creates a sclerotic structure that impairs our judgement. We end up providing the *right* answer to the *wrong* question. A more interesting question than how we select between right and wrong is how we apply our truest desire to the chaos of the world.

The tension between Chaos and Eros finds expression at times in popular culture. Take, for example, Stephen Sondheim's musical *A Little Night Music*, a brilliant adaptation of Ingmar Bergman's film *Smiles of a Summer Night*. The characters are facing the chaos that is their lives – the failed relationships, the missed opportunities. Probably the musical's most famous and poignant song is performed by Desiree (incidentally, the French word for "desired") at a time when she is reflecting on her past affair with Fredrik, who, like Desiree, lives in an unhappy relationship but will not leave his wife for her. This is "Send in the Clowns". Sondheim shows typical genius in conjuring up the image of the clown, in order to help Desiree, down on the ground, deal with her own confrontation with the Abyss, whereas the object of her *desire* lives up in mid-air, closer to Eros.

In my childhood when my parents took me to the local circus, I always enjoyed the interaction between the two clowns: the white clown, always serious and reasonable, and his comical and colourful sidekick. I am surprised when I hear that some of my adult (and otherwise extremely balanced!) friends still nourish a deep aversion toward clowns to this day. Why is the image of the clown so strongly evocative?

In the Greek theatre of antiquity, clowns were represented as rustic buffoons (we find these again centuries later in the *Commedia dell'arte*). At the time, they were known as *pantomimos* (meaning "imitators of all"), *deikeliktas* ("those who put on plays") or *sklero-paiktes* ("those who play like children"). The reason clowns appeal so much to children is because they draw on the same mix of child-like energies: unleashed creativity combined with puerile recklessness.

I recently heard of a French benevolent association called Clowns Z'hôpitaux, which sends some of its volunteers to children's wards in hospitals, to distract them from their pains and worries, even if only for a short time. The association's spokesperson commented on the joint act between the White (sad) Clown and the Auguste (happy) Clown as a metaphor for our different attitudes to chaos.

The White Clown remains rational in front of the inevitable, and is disillusioned – whereas the Auguste Clown, who applies fantasy to the chaos he faces, may get hurt along the way but is invariably the winner in the end.

I suppose we are all partly White Clown, partly Auguste Clown, especially when the prospect of facing chaos makes us feel as ill-equipped as the children we once were. Hence, we need to make sure that we don't hand over the keys only to the rational White Clown, and that we keep engaging with our own inner Auguste. Incidentally, the word Auguste itself stems from the Latin for "consecrated by the augurs; with favourable auguries" – perhaps an incentive to take him seriously and ignore the heavy make-up and red noses!

ORIENTATION POINT

Desire and Chaos work together to create the volatile environment in which we all operate. The best decision-makers are those who respond lightly to chaos, wherever possible, rather than imagining they can still its turbulence by a large measure of reason. The Auguste Clown, in folk tale, offers a way of dealing with chaos effectively – through creativity.
Be creative and accepting, rather than fearful and resistant, and you are likelier to prevail.

Finally, fear of failure may be linked to the fear of the consequences of risk, not so much on ourselves, but rather on others. In other words, we may be infected by the fear of disappointing them – whether as partner, parent, offspring, colleague, friend, or in any other capacity.

However, we are often wrong about how they are thinking. So, not only are we overly focused on other people's judgement, but our perception of their expectations is also distorted by bias.

A few years ago, at a gathering of young bankers, I heard their Managing Director tell them that although mistakes may be disappointing, what was more disappointing to him was people not trying, not taking risks, albeit calculated ones. "Ultimately," he said, "I'm successful in this business because I'm right 51 per cent of the time!"

How wonderful would it be if every child could hear a similar message from their parents: "I'd rather you tried and failed, than for you not to try. Not trying, not giving it a go, and therefore – if we pursue this thought logically – not allowing yourself to fail: these are the only things that could disappoint me."

I recently met with another client, an Irish entrepreneur still in his 40s, who was about to sell his company. He is a self-made man who built a highly successful and attractive business. Surely he must know a thing or two about effective decision making, I thought. So I asked him what his secret was. He answered that he owed his success to his first boss, who offered some wise words when as a young employee he faced his first difficult choices: "If you make a decision, I'll be fine whatever the outcome. However, if you don't decide, I'll have to fire you."

When facing the chaos of tough decisions and all their possible outcomes, our first inclination may well be to drag our heels, stall and end up firmly rooted to the ground. Yet we need to look up and seek in our true desire – in Eros, high in the sky – the resources to transform chaos into a new reality. Our desire itself has two aspects to it: the rational side and the more childlike, playful, creative side. It is only by engaging all these resources that we can break the deadlock, caused by our fear of failure and our indecision.

2 Fear of heights

At the opposite end of the spectrum to *fear of failure* is *fear of heights*. This is the fear that sets in when we ask ourselves: what if it works? What if I pass my exams? What if I meet the right person for me? What if I win the lottery? What if I'm successful? What if I do find my own voice in my creative work?

Whereas rationally we would expect these positive prospects to fill us with joy, they may also create their own flavour of anxiety. That is because success, whatever form it takes, will create its own demands. It may also set us free, and if you remember the earlier story of the modern-day slaves (see page 6), you will know how, once liberated, they often find themselves unable to make even the most basic decisions. This applies to many of us when we face the prospect of succeeding, and of our minds being set free. Rather than accepting the challenge of freedom, we may end up preferring the comfort of inaction, a bit like the anti-hero of Dostoyevsky's *Notes from the Underground*, who says:

> "Why has [man] such a passionate love for destruction and chaos also? [...] May it not be that he loves chaos and destruction [...] because he is instinctively afraid of attaining his object and completing the edifice he is constructing?[...] Perhaps the only goal on earth to which mankind is striving is in this incessant process of attaining, in other words, in life itself, and not in the thing to be attained, which must always be expressed as a formula, as positive as twice two makes four, and such positiveness is not life, gentlemen, but it is the beginning of death."

Once again, this time in the company of Dostoyevsky, we revisit the daunting space on the upper edge of the abyss, somewhere between choice and chaos. What Dostoyevsky teaches us is that the fear of heights is not a fear of vertigo (what happens *once* I'm up there, once I have achieved my goals?) but a fear of achievement (what happens *when* I get up there? Where do I go next?). Grasping at last the object of our quest, in his opinion, coincides with the beginning of death. In this, he echoes Dante's view that "the worst inferno is to be surfeited with what we seek".

What Dostoyevsky highlights is that fear of heights is not necessarily linked to (metaphorical) altitude; instead it is linked to time. The Greeks had two separate notions for time: *chronos* and *kairos*.

From a *chronos* point of view, wherein each second has the same weight and time flows in a linear way, the punctual moment when we achieve our goals is almost accidental. However, from a *kairos* point of view it is very significant – for *kairos* does not measure time quantitatively (that is, chronologically) but qualitatively. The word itself means "opportune moment, perfect moment". Dostoyevsky's anti-hero is not concerned with the height of the edifice, or the moment in *chronos* when he reaches its peak. His concern is about *kairos*: where does reaching the summit leave him?

ORIENTATION POINT

The moment of attaining a goal after taking the decision to strive for it ought to be one of triumph. However, we need to beware of it feeling empty – an anti-climax, because success is not life-changing after all; or perhaps it will lead to a life change we are ill-equipped to cope with. Sometimes we may even hold back from a decision because we know in advance that we lack the resources to deal with the impact of success.

This points to two dangers: the first one happens when we ignore *kairos* and live with the deluded sense of time as merely chrono(*chronos*)logical. This can lead us to procrastination, because in the chronological world tomorrow is similar to today: another day of 24 hours, a mere "D+1" to today's "D". In this world of *chronos* and procrastination (*crastinus* means "belonging to tomorrow"), we feel that time is entirely outside us. We all know people whose lives follow the monotonously predictable pace dictated by *chronos* – whereby easy decisions happen in the present and challenging choices are postponed to another day, because tomorrow is an *ideal* space, and therefore always seems to offer the best potential for things to turn out ideally. These people miss a sense of *kairos*, the idea that there is such a thing as an ideal timing for things to happen, a serendipitous moment when our stars are aligned. In their world – a world without *kairos* – every moment is treated as if it were a rehearsal for life itself. Here we encounter the illusory belief that postponing a decision until tomorrow is without consequences, that it will not affect the person or their decisions.

Unfortunately, we know this is not the case. Procrastination is not the refusal to decide, to "freeze" a decision in time, it is the decision to remain undecided. For this reason, as I've already suggested, procrastination doesn't postpone the pains of decision to another, remote day: instead, it multiplies that pain by spreading it across every minute of every day, between now and then.

ORIENTATION POINT

Procrastination perpetuates undecidedness, which is an intrinsically unsatisfactory experience. You may think you are putting off the agony of choice, but in fact you are extending that agony into the future. Procrastination weighs upon the spirit just as an unfulfilled duty weighs upon the conscience.

The opposite danger is to dwell in *kairos*, to bask in the glory of our achievements, and to look down on the world, animated by an irrepressible feeling of superiority. This is *kairos* without *chronos*; it is also what Dostoyevsky's character refers to as "the beginning of death". I'm reminded of a play I saw at the National Theatre, called *People, Places and Things*, in which Emma, a drug addict, uses a Wile E Coyote metaphor to describe her addiction: "Wile E Coyote only ever falls when he looks down. He runs off the cliff and just keeps running in mid-air. It's only when he looks down and sees that he should be falling that gravity kicks in."

The same is true of our decisions. We experience life when we enact our choices, but it does not last if we start feeling the fear of heights, and look down: then gravity kicks in. James Hollis writes that "Fear is the enemy – most of all, fear of largeness. The largeness of our own soul is most intimidating, which is why we defer so often to the instructions of others."

3 Fear of identification

Another variant of counterproductive fear may be illustrated by an excursion into art history. Leonardo da Vinci's early work the *Adoration of the Magi* (c1481) hangs in the Uffizi Gallery in Florence – as does his *Annunciation* (c1472). These are two of the gallery's most precious pictures.

Leonardo received the commission to paint the *Adoration* by the friars of San Donato a Scopeto in Florence, but he left for Milan the following year (1482), leaving the painting unfinished.

When Pope Sixtus IV commissioned the painting of the walls of the Vatican chapel in Rome that bears his name, the Sistine Chapel, he enlisted the most talented artists of the time, among them Botticelli, Perugino, Pinturicchio, Ghirlandaio. They were joined, under his successors Pope Julius II and Leo X, by Michelangelo, who decorated the world-famous ceiling, and Raphael who designed the tapestries and the private apartments.

However, one name was missing from this enterprise, perhaps the most prominent artist of them all: Leonardo da Vinci. By then, Leonardo had already acquired a well-deserved reputation, not just for the inimitable quality of his works, but also, more problematically, for not finishing his commissions. The *Adoration of the Magi* was only the most recent iteration of a familiar story. And neither Pope Sixtus nor his successors were prepared to take a risk on that scale.

Where did Leonardo's questionable reputation stem from? After all, this is the prolific genius who revolutionized not only the arts (with inventions like *sfumato*, a technique for softening colours, in painting) but also many scientific disciplines, as evidenced by the hundreds of pages we have inherited in his five codices.

One explanation for Leonardo's many unfinished works lies in some disastrous experiments with new painting techniques and materials. In the case of the *Last Supper*, which he painted on one wall of the refectory of the church of Santa Maria delle Grazie in Milan, the first signs of decay started to appear less than 20 years after its completion.

However, this is only one part of the story. The other reason why Leonardo left many works unfinished is that if they failed to show the early promise of becoming masterpieces – realizing this, he would swiftly move on to new projects.

Leonardo once wrote that his paintings were already finished in his mind, before he started working on them. Occasionally, this would lead him to create some of the most beautiful and memorable paintings in history, but his vision did not always materialize as intended. And he was famous for destroying any sketches or drawings that disappointed him.

What haunted Leonardo was the fear of completing a work that he anticipated would fail to meet his own standards. He preferred admitting early defeat, rather than leaving these "inferior" works hanging in public places or private palaces for people to see and criticize. The fear was that he would be forever associated with works of art he felt were not worthy of him.

This is the fear of identification – the belief that any criticism of what we have created is a criticism of the intrinsic self. Our inner voice tells us: you are what you do. And it isn't only our inner voice: our parents, teachers, managers, clients and so on may well have uttered the same refrain.

When I was a student, I took a job as an intern at a London investment bank. I remember that one of my senior colleagues had pinned a colour A4 print-out of the *Mona Lisa* on her office wall, captioned by the words: "Treat every piece of work you do as if it were your self-portrait." I was not sure at the time whether to feel inspired or horrified by this message.

With hindsight, I choose the latter response. Identification with our work, and more generally with our actions, is a common source of fear, impeding effective decision making. The fear, for many people, generates enormous stress and anxiety. This is another reason why we sometimes procrastinate around whether we should or shouldn't take on a project: we worry that our name will forever be associated with the enterprise, which will in some way define us; and in doing so it will also necessarily limit us.

Such limitation marks the incarceration of the Self by the ego. At some level, we are aware of the risk that the limits imposed in this way will compromise our potential, weakening our life force.

Moreover, this limitation reduces our scope by creating artificial boundaries for us. Hence, the fear of identification is also a fear of narrowness.

Carl Jung once humorously remarked that we all walk in shoes too small for us. "Living within a constricted view of our journey," writes James Hollis, "and resorting to old defensive strategies, we unwittingly become the enemies of our own growth, our own largeness of soul ..." We live repetitively, rather than breaking out for new ground. Our decision making becomes timid.

For Hollis, the fundamental problem lies in our identification with the "false self" (a term coined by Donald Winnicott). This is made up of "the values and strategies we have derived from internalizing the dynamics of our family and our culture." The false self is what stops us from achieving the largeness of soul we should all aim for.

Ultimately, I believe the identification we should fear most is not an identification with our actions, but with that fake part of ourselves, which usurps our authentic souls and muffles the most meaningful and deepest expression of who we are.

> ## ORIENTATION POINT
>
> The best decision making emerges when we allow ourselves to be authentic. Worrying about how a decision, or its consequences, will make us appear to others is likely to result in poor choices, and will rob us of any prospect of true fulfilment.

The false self can also project an overly expansive rather than reductive view of our journey. This is what happens when it makes us look at certain opportunities as "beneath us". It originates from a feeling of self-importance, which is usually of a compensatory nature – we only compensate for those things we fear we may be missing. So, feeling that a project is unworthy of our efforts probably reflects a fear that we may fall short of what life requires from us.

Fear of identification is therefore something we should remain on our guard about, whenever we feel uneasy about making a decision. If we fear our endeavours will bear our own indelible stamp, let us remember that the alternative is surely worse: not putting your stamp on things, and as a result becoming invisible, insignificant, easily forgotten.

4 Fear of lack of recognition

As fear is mostly irrational, one type of fear can easily flip into its opposite. We may be subject to a fear of identification, but we may just as easily succumb to its flipside: a fear of lack of recognition. This is what happens when, for example, we approach a project we intend to take on but at the last minute are seized by doubts along the lines of: why am I doing this? is this really for me? why should I even bother? why can't the others do it? The fear is that a project that is not truly ours will use our time and energy and, as a result, distract us from our own personal agenda. This is also the fear of being taken for granted, of being disrespected.

My view is that, if we genuinely owned our personal agenda, this question would not occur to us. People who have a clear idea of what they are about, and what path they are on, do not face this conundrum. They are able to say "no" without guilt and "yes" without resentment. Those who do feel the guilt of refusal are not only – and not essentially – expressing remorse over how their choice may affect others. The much greater, deeper guilt comes from their feeling that in not owning their agenda, they have betrayed themselves.

Conversely, of course, you might choose to say "yes" rather than "no" – in which case an inner resentment might build up: you resent yourself for passively accepting something which is in someone else's interest, not yours. You are a long way here from the kind of joy that stems from selfless giving.

Paradoxically, the greater consciousness we have of our own agenda, and the greater our ease with ourselves on that account, the more likely we are to welcome being distracted from it.

This is why empathy is so powerful. Empathy distracts us from our own agenda to pay due attention to others. Empathy is spontaneous, it cannot be part of a calculated plan, or of *any* agenda. Moreover, empathy is what creates connection.

ORIENTATION POINT

Decision making is often a narrowly personal operation: we have our agenda and we seek to make decisions that advance it. However, a fully rounded person will always allow empathy to enter the field of play. Typically, we become acutely aware of another person's perspective, projecting ourselves into their predicament. When this modifies our decision making, that shows the triumph of connection over self-interest.

On this topic, the author and researcher Brené Brown describes how vulnerability may be one of our greatest fears, driving many other fears including the one under consideration here – the fear of not being recognized. Yet this vulnerability can also be seen as an asset; it is intimately bound up with empathy, and enriches us by enlarging our emotional horizons.

A world without empathy would be a chilling place to live, with all of us separate from each other, trapped in the cold ice of disconnection. This is the image used by Dante in Canto XXXII of his Inferno to describe

Cocytus, the Ninth Circle of Hell, located at the bottom of the Abyss. "As they denied God's love, so are they furthest removed from the light and warmth of His Sun. As they denied all human ties, so are they bound only by the unyielding ice."

5 Fear of selfishness

If we elect to live in a world of connection, we may yet have to face one further fear: that of upsetting others, or of being perceived as acting in a selfish manner.

Granted, we cannot expect each and every one of our acts to benefit people around us. At the same time, our path cannot be constantly obstructed by this concern. Only by being grounded in our own personality can we truly be of service to others. What is most needed here is a healthy awareness of our own boundaries and a clear understanding of our own psychological cartography: the terrain that is shared with others and the terrain that is ours alone.

Moreover, there is a great difference between people *feeling* hurt by something we say or do and people *being* hurt. We are not responsible for people's emotional states, only for our own acts and intentions, and for ensuring that we do not wilfully or negligently cause harm.

Carl Jung drew this simple symbol of the human psyche, where the outside circle represents the Self (*Selbst*) and the central dot the ego (*Ich*):

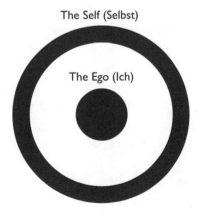

The Self (Selbst)

The Ego (Ich)

Self is the Jungian archetype representing the unification of consciousness and unconsciousness in a person, and is realized as a result of individuation – moving toward wholeness. *Ich* is the German word for "I", as well as for the psychoanalytical concept of "ego".

We need the alignment of Self and ego to function as human beings, with a strong sense of ego – the centre of our consciousness – at the core of our psychological make-up. Only by making, not selfish but "Self-Ich" decisions, with the ego grounded in the midst of the Self, can we be truly altruistic. If we can manage this, the act of caring for others becomes a gift that elevates us rather than a sacrifice we may resent.

The opposite happens when we say to others: "I want *you* to choose." This could even be offensive if it implies that "I'm big enough that I can selflessly give you what you want, whereas I'm not convinced you have the same ability." Moreover, if it truly fills me with pleasure to let you have your way, why would I deprive you of the same benefit?

If both parties are unsure about the best action plan, delegating a decision to someone else is just an uncomfortable and cowardly way of making the other person answerable for its consequences.

Ultimately, delegation of will, when it does not come from a strong and centred sense of ego, is likely to be a sign of passivity ("you, because you are other, are better qualified than me to decide"), of passive aggression ("we might as well do it your way") or of grandiosity ("I, uniquely, have it in my power to provide others with joy"). These are three of the least assertive, least self-affirming behaviours.

In summary, fear of selfishness only has a place in our lives if we have grounds to believe that our character is truly selfish. The only acceptable solution then is not to overrule our decisions, but gently to tend to our psyches, and start exploring the kind of joy that comes from giving without expectations.

6 Beyond fear

To complete our review of the fears associated with decision making, we should note that there are two additional tendencies to reflect on. Our fears can be exacerbated by either of these powerful engines: the "fear of fear" and the "thrill of fear".

Another expression for "fear of fear" could be simply "panic". We know we are in its thrall when our response to a threat is incommensurate to the threat itself. If I don't like driving, the panic I may feel before taking the wheel is likely to be a fear of the state I am in, rather than an actual fear of driving.

The same applies to our decisions – and this is particularly noticeable in the case of our most trivial decisions, such as picking a restaurant for lunch or what to order once we are seated at the restaurant we ended up booking. Because these are not life-changing decisions, the anxiety that accompanies them is likely to be prompted by the fear of *making* a bad choice, rather than by the choice itself, and its likely *outcome*. Panic makes us confuse the former with the latter. Under its spell, the fear of deciding between two equally valid options overdramatizes the dilemma.

Of course, fear of fear also applies to more extreme situations. These include the "fear of all fears", or in other words, the fear of death. Obviously, few decisions are a matter of life or death, but at the same time some people will object that because our time on Earth is finite, we must be careful and economical with the decisions we make; and, for example, the fear of missing out could be related to the feeling that time is running out, and that an opportunity will not present itself again, irrespective of whether the opportunity itself is good for us in the first place.

Underlying this attitude – the opposite of *carpe diem* ("seize the day"), and probably more like *serva diem* ("preserve the day") – is the thought that in an ideal world, if we could live forever, we would not need to worry about our decisions, because we could try everything and never fear a negative outcome. But would life really be like this?

At this stage, it's worth briefly exploring how people cope when they are not under the pressure imposed by mortality. We may not be able to encounter many immortals, but we can reflect on the fate, in mythology and literature, of those characters who receive the gift of eternal life.

In Greek mythology, immortality features in the dramatic stories of Prometheus, Narcissus and Tithonus. The latter found immortality so unbearable that he begged the gods to make him mortal.

Much closer to us, in his short story *The Immortal*, Jorge Luis Borges explores the idea that life derives its true meaning from death. The story is about an entire society which, having achieved immortality, loses its motivation for any action.

At the other end of the spectrum we have Wolfgang Amadeus Mozart, who dated his creative genius back to the time when he became aware, early in his short life, of his own mortality.

The opposite of *fear of fear* is *thrill of fear*. This is very different from the thrill of deciding. With the latter, we feel excitement about the prospect of a positive outcome. The thrill of fear, however, is an excitement generated by an irrational element and the fear it provokes. It is a type of addiction. Under its spell, people may not have problems making decisions, but they may well have problems dealing with their consequences. If in doubt, ask gamblers and City traders for their views!

Having visited each of the seven fears, and their derivatives, we are bound to wonder where this leaves us. In fact, on the brink of decision making, we are facing a securely locked door – we have not yet been given the key, only some clues as to how we could so easily fail, through one of the fears, to put our hands on it.

Further guidance follows. However, in our quest toward answers, you may find it tempting to peep through the keyhole of that door, to see what lies on the other side. The door's lock is the outside circle in Jung's drawing of the human psyche, and the keyhole is the ego, the black dot in the centre of the circle.

Jung claimed that the conflicts we experience in our lives are often reflections of conflicts within our own psyches; and for this reason, they can lead us to a better understanding of ourselves.

So, what happens when we look from here – from the outside – into the room through the prism of our whole psyche? What can we see inside, beyond fear? Having gained first-hand experience of looking through this lock, I, for one, can confess that there's exciting news, but there's also less enthusing ones.

The good news is that there is definitely light visible, which gives us confidence that the path is right. But we must brace ourselves. For immediately beyond fear, there are further challenges to be faced.

CHAPTER 4

THROUGH THE LOOKING GLASS

In *Through the Looking-Glass*, the sequel to *Alice's Adventures in Wonderland*, the young heroine climbs through a mirror into a fantastic world populated by surreal creatures, where everything is inverted, even logic. There, Alice finds a book written in a seemingly cryptic language, but she is able to read its reversed lettering by holding it up to the mirror.

On the other side of the metaphorical door and keyhole, there is – in the realm of our decision making – an inverted world awaiting us. The fears to be found there are not the same fears examined in the previous chapter, but their reverse projections, seen through the Self-ego "keyhole". In other words, the fears of decision making we have identified are reflections of more numerous and deeper fears within us, originating from early childhood. According to the Jungian analyst James Hollis, these fears fall into two broad categories: the fear of insufficiency or abandonment (fear of not enough) and its opposite, the fear of engulfment (fear of too much). Moreover, it is important to note that this applies to all of us, not only to people with psychological issues.

For example, the fear of failure described earlier can be the translation of the deeper fear of insufficiency. Often we may feel that as a result of failure, we will be lacking in something that is crucial to us – affection, time, opportunity, money, security. At the same time, we may worry that our failure will make us dependent on others, and will subject us to engulfment – the overwhelming of the Self.

Where during childhood your psyche has been affected by the experience and internalization of engulfment/insufficiency anxieties, it is likely that in later life you will seek to overcompensate for what has been lacking. For example, a child who has not received enough affection may become clingy in their adult relationships or suffer from a feeling of unworthiness.

When it comes to decision making, if we are stuck in a similar pattern (what Freud called "repetition compulsion"), we may suddenly find that every decision seems labelled with the words "mission impossible".

This explains why we need to break free from such patterns and enlarge our consciousness. The risk, otherwise, is that we grow into a false sense of self-identity, and as a result get caught in what psychologists Jeffery E Young and Janet S Klosko call "life traps".

They have identified, through their research, eleven such places where we may get stuck. Once we have fallen prey to one of these life traps, we end up recreating later in life the very conditions of our childhood that were most harmful to us.

The 11 life traps are:

- *Abandonment* Fear of being abandoned by your partner or someone else important to you.

- *Mistrust/abuse* You mistrust others or tend to find yourself in abusive situations.

- *Emotional deprivation* You feel you will never obtain the love you need.

- *Dependence* You feel unable to keep going without having someone to look after you.

- *Defectiveness* You feel there is something seriously wrong with you, though you might not know quite what it is.

- *Social exclusion* You feel like an outsider, unable to fit in well with everyone else.

- *Failure* You feel you yourself are a failure, based on your poor track record for success.

- *Entitlement* You feel that the world owes you something.

- *Subjugation* You feel controlled by other people.

- *Vulnerability* You feel something terrible is likely to happen to you personally.

- *Unrelenting standards* You feel you must push yourself constantly, allowing no time for rest or enjoyment.

Identifying "where", if anywhere, we are stuck is an essential first step toward growing out of our narrow vision of the world and expanding into the largeness of our souls. Blinkered by too narrow a perspective, we find that good decisions are beyond us. But once the horizons of the self expand in this way, wonderful new choices become available.

By this stage, we have established the following:

- The fears related to decision making can hide other, deeper fears inherited from childhood.
- There are two childhood fears – engulfment and insufficiency – which taint our vision of the world, and pervade our other fears.
- Unless we address any issues of engulfment and insufficiency, we run the risk of remaining stuck in one or more of the 11 life traps.

We know from TV drama that a good detective can solve a crime by latching on to what appeared to everyone else as an irrelevant detail.

If I don my rumpled old detective mac for a moment, I cannot fail to notice that there is an uncanny complementarity between our seven fears of decision making and the eleven life traps. For example, the fear of selfishness hides a greater fear of rejection (for being selfish) and therefore of being caught in the "social exclusion" life trap.

ORIENTATION POINT

To identify faulty or fearful decision making with psychic wounds inherited from childhood may seem relevant only to a small portion of the population: those perhaps who might benefit from therapy. In fact, however, these wounds are commonplace, and can affect all of us. Our decision making can certainly be improved if we are honest enough to probe our own insecurities.

The Seven Fears of Decision Making	What they say	What they may hide
Rejecting a better option	"I might miss out."	"I will be missed out, ie rejected."
Choosing the wrong option	"There may be something wrong with this choice."	"There is something wrong with me."
Failure	"This undertaking may be a failure."	"I am a failure."
Heights	"These things might all collapse."	"I will break down."
Identification	"This idea probably says a lot about me."	"My life is empty."
Lack of recognition	"I may not be valued for this."	"I am not worthy."
Selfishness	"Maybe I will come across as selfish."	"I am selfish."

However, the seven fears we have explored are about decisions – whereas life traps are about us, our own personalities, the way we conduct ourselves inwardly. This realization provides us with an important key. Could it be that the fears of decision making, once seen through Jung's drawing of the psyche (which, you'll no doubt remember, I referred to irreverently as a lock and keyhole), are really fears about ourselves? And could it be that the language they hide, behind the language they actually use, is really something like the table above.

These are the deep layers of fear we can identify through the keyhole. They can also be seen as insights: they tell us why, when we need to make a decision, our psyche occasionally applies the brakes at the very moment we want it to shift up a gear.

Therefore, peeping through the keyhole is not enough. If we want our decision making to get truly under way and move in the right direction, we will need to unlock the door and tread the path that awaits us on the other side. This is where we explore the territory where our will gets stuck. It is also where we answer the question, *Where art thou?*

KEY SKILL I

HOW TO MANAGE RISK

"We are bound to accept that engaging in decision making involves the acceptance of risk as a key part of the equation." (see page 40)

To live a life without risk would be a cheerless prospect, however idyllic the idea might seem at first sight. Eventually the sense of missed opportunities would start to nibble away at your well-being. You would castigate yourself for inertia, for not finding suitable outlets for your talents. Nobody would see you as a worthwhile companion for an adventure. Your stock among your peers would sink in value. You would wither morally and spiritually.

In the business world, risk is often seen as a price that rises in proportion to the reward. Risk too much and you are betting for wealth beyond measure against what you would be profoundly reluctant to lose; risk too little and you end up with the equivalent of small change.

A healthy attitude to risk is one that is based on awareness (knowing what is at stake, what the rewards are and having a good sense of how likely you are to achieve them) and on courage (resilience against failure, and ideally some sense of relish in the challenge).

Four responses
When a risk is identified, you are faced with four clear options: accept, reduce, transfer or avoid. Acceptance is best undertaken after you have reduced the risk as much as possible without diminishing the reward too much. Transferring the risk means involving others in your enterprise – for example, finding a financial backer. Avoidance means either accepting the current situation instead of deciding on a risky new adventure, or else looking for a safer method of changing what is unsatisfactory about the status quo.

An effective, fully motivated business person will move toward his or her vision knowing there will be failures on the way, often requiring an improvised change of strategy. Failure teaches better than success. Moving one way, then another, as the direction of travel is re-orientated in response to evolving circumstances is all part of the growth experience – both personal and collective.

Learning to divest the word "failure" of its overtones of shame is a key skill for anyone in business. In the therapy of neuro-linguistic programming (NLP), subjects are taught that there is no such thing as failure, only feedback. Terminology is a matter of personal choice, but certainly it is healthy to be able to speak of a **project** failing without any tinge of embarrassment – though unhealthy to speak of a person failing.

All-round thinking

In any situation of business risk, it is good to have contingency and mitigation plans in place. All possible eventualities should be considered. Some managers may speak of the "unthinkable", but this is dangerous talk, for two important reasons:

- The worst possible outcomes are precisely those that should be faced unflinchingly, not pushed aside as catastrophes no one is willing to contemplate.
- Labelling an outcome "unthinkable" inevitably makes people think disaster has occurred if ever that outcome should come to pass – whereas satisfactory contingency plans should ideally make the worst-case scenario something everyone can live with.

Risk management should in fact be a key part of every project. Seeking views from people with relevant experience is an essential part of the assessment process. Also important is communication: all too often the manager of a project is not properly briefed on the risks by those he or she reports to. Any sponsors should also be involved in the communication loop.

It is important too to clarify who **owns** the risk. If this is apparent from the beginning, the risks are likely to be better monitored and controlled. Conversely, if there is no clarity on this matter, one of the consequences of failure is likely to be a miasma of confusion and blame.

A final point worth stressing is that any undertaking has built-in opportunities as well as risks, and both should be scrutinized equally. Ignoring the possible upsides while focusing only on possible downsides is an imbalanced approach that serves no one's interests. You need to plan what happens if things go right as well as if things go wrong – the art of positive contingency. Any time spent looking at how to make the most of bonus outcomes is thoroughly worthwhile.

KEY SKILL 2

HOW TO ATTAIN DETACHMENT

"Only by being grounded in our own personality can we truly be of service to others." (see page 51)

"Detachment" is a word fraught with complications. The job of the individual in a business context is usually to act for the collective interest rather than, for example, to further their own career. That does not mean caring about your career is wrong – only that actively filling the role you have agreed to take on involves re-aligning your personal interests and maybe at times de-prioritizing them.

Hidden motivations

Such an approach is easier said than done. One complicating factor is the way personal motivations often lurk below the surface of the mind, influencing decision making without our knowledge. There may be unconscious bias at work. Examples, in addition to career furtherance (how your decision will appear to those with the power to favour you), include:

- Personality preferences – for example, choosing to deal with someone you like rather than the optimum person, who may be temperamentally problematic in some way.
- Speed of outcome – impatience to see results, and gain credit for them, may militate against the choice of an outcome that is better for your company in the long run. Conversely, you might opt for a slow outcome if you know you will not be around when its worst aspects come to light.
- Ease of obtaining support – this is really a form of peer pressure. You know your preferred choice runs the risk of floundering through lack of support, so you opt for Realpolitik instead of idealism.

Shades of grey

In all these instances there will be different ways of looking at the situation. A personality preference may be valid if good communication is of prime importance. A particular pace of outcome may have benefits institutionally as well as for yourself. And there is usually no point in making a choice you know will be voted down – although if everyone thought like that, nothing exceptional would be achieved.

Again, personal bias comes into play. How you see your motivation – best for everyone or best for yourself – is a choice you can make either way. Ruthless honesty with yourself, aligning the ego more closely with the Self in a mature and considered view of any complexities, is vital if you seek to act as disinterestedly as possible.

The dimension of values

Personal values come into the picture. Only by following your own values can you be said to be acting authentically; and authenticity is an important part of the toolkit you are using on others' behalf. When you were recruited to the job or role, it was the whole you that was signed up. The moral self and the executive self cannot be separated. Yet they can sometimes find themselves at loggerheads with each other.

In particular, an occasional pitfall in business is to override the individual in favour of the bottom line. An obvious example would be the case of a manager who is asked to let go an employee who has been loyal to the company, for reasons entirely extraneous to his or her performance – for example, because of a drive to cut costs owing to a market downturn.

To navigate such complexities, it is wise to create your own code of ethics and consult this before making business decisions. This is the kind of bias that must never be ignored. Consider the impact of your decisions on **all** stakeholders. Consult others when making decisions that have wide ramifications, as your personal viewpoint may be too narrow to grasp these, however empathic you are. Review the outcome of your past decision making and learn from any mistakes you have made – being blind to your own mistakes is a bias that will always compromise future outcomes.

PART II
WHERE ART THOU?

CHAPTER 5

SELF STARTERS

"Perhaps all the dragons in our lives are princesses who are only waiting to see us act, just once, with beauty and courage. Perhaps everything that frightens us is, in its deepest essence, something helpless that wants our love."

Rainer Maria Rilke, *Letters to a Young Poet*

Let us take stock of where the first phase of our exploration has taken us. We started with the symptoms of indecision. We then dug further into the defence mechanisms and the fears holding us back – only to realize that those fears mirror deeper fears about the Self. We ended the previous section with the Self, and this is also where we will start this new one – hence the title of the present chapter.

Part I finished with the threats to the Self, whereby the Self is a potential "victim". Part II now starts with the Self as "agent" – the Self as part of the solution, not part of the problem.

In other words: we ended Part I addressing the fears of the *implication* of our decisions *on the Self*; we shall now shift to the subject of the *implication of the Self* in our decisions.

The word "implication" has two different meanings:

- Involving someone or something in the nature or operation of something – for example, when someone is implicated in a project, and we expect them to deliver results.
- Bringing into incriminating connection – for example, when someone is implicated in a crime, based on the available evidence.

Accordingly, if the Self is implicated in decisions, it has to be:

• Responsible, as an active agent.
• Answerable and accountable for the consequences of a decision.

I believe that behind any lack of decisiveness, there is a lack of implication of the Self.

For example, we often hear that good leaders are not afraid of making bad decisions. I suggest that what this really means is: they are not afraid of implicating themselves (that is, their Selves), nor are they afraid of the implications of a bad decision for them (that is, for their egos). Instead, they view this as one of the risks they should be prepared to accept as leaders; and accordingly they make sure that they are fully engaged in driving through their decisions. This implies they will stand behind their decisions, whatever the consequences. It does not exclude the possibility of revisiting a decision if it turns out – or looks likely to turn out – differently from the way it was intended. However, even in this scenario, they will not disown the initial decision. Their implication is simultaneously total and final.

A word we came across earlier is "conundrum", which in my experience is not a word used by many leaders. They prefer speaking about "difficult", "challenging", "tough" or "hard" decisions. A conundrum is a choice that isn't grounded in the Self. Etymologically, a conundrum is a whim. It tends to lead to shallow decision making.

At the extreme end, a conundrum becomes a "Cornelian choice", or "Cornelian dilemma", after the 17th-century French dramatist Pierre Corneille. In this daunting scenario, the protagonists must choose between two courses of action, either of which will have a disastrous impact on them or someone close to them. This is what awaits Rodrigue, the hero of Corneille's play *Le Cid*, who needs to decide between the love of Chimène or the honour of his family, which has been wronged by Chimène's father – a tough decision between, on the one hand, revenge without love, and, on the other, love without revenge!

What can we learn from such tragedies? According to the Jungian analyst James Hollis, the common thread between them is *self-estrangement*. Hollis describes how this is the subject matter of Greek tragedies, where the protagonist makes flawed choices on the basis of limited self-knowledge. A "wounded vision of self and world" leads to bad decisions and bad consequences. Such experience is universal and timeless, with plentiful examples in modern life.

At the heart of these tragic situations is lack of awareness and lack of implication of the Self. This is not a matter of the intentional withdrawal of the Self from a situation, but the painful realization that the Self has deserted us when it was most needed. The space vacated by the Self is then occupied by its readily-available ersatz, the "false self".

We are all vulnerable to falling for the allure of the false self, but the price we pay for our attraction to the fake part of us is self-estrangement, with all its damaging consequences.

The 1966 science fiction film *Seconds*, by John Frankenheimer, tells the story of Arthur Hamilton, a middle-aged suburban banker who has had a successful and rewarding career but feels unhappy with both his private and professional lives. He is approached by a secret organization that allows him to start a new life, by giving him the body of a young man (played by Rock Hudson) through advanced medical technology. From then on, Hamilton, who is presumed dead, lives a life much more glamorous and exciting than anything he has experienced before. But he is still dissatisfied. The film ends by making it clear that no attempt to fix the outer self could do anything to address the inner self's crisis. It is implied too that once the false self has crashed, the authentic self is equally doomed. For Hamilton, they both vanish.

Self-estrangement implies that the Self has separated from us – that it is hiding from us, or vice versa. We must therefore undertake a search for it, wherever it resides, down to its darkest lairs.

The shortest question in the Bible is, remarkably, God's first question. In Genesis 3.9, Adam and Eve have just eaten the forbidden fruit and, aware of God's presence, they hide behind the trees. At this moment, God asks Adam a simple question: "Where are you?" In Hebrew the question is even shorter, in fact just one word: *Ayeka?*

In the very *first* book of the Bible, God addresses the *first* man of his creation with the *first* and most essential question, in just *one* word meaning "where are you?" Naturally, we can assume that God knows full well where Adam is physically hiding: his question is about Adam's essential nature.

In *The Way of Man*, the Austrian-born philosopher Martin Buber reflects on the meaning of this question: "In every era, God calls to every man: 'Where are you in your world? So many years and days of those allotted to you have passed, and how far have you gotten in your world? [...] How far along are you?'" This is also an essential question we should be asking ourselves. Where are we really, in our personal (that is, social, psychological, spiritual, intellectual and moral) growth? At the same time, if and when we feel stuck, where are we hiding?

Hiding gives us a fake sense of safety. In the childhood game of "hide-and-seek" we may have found a clever hiding place, but we have relinquished any form of control and it is surely only a matter of time before the seeker finds us. As I am currently writing this chapter in Italy, I am reminded by my Roman friends that the Italian expression for the game of "hide-and-seek" is *cacciare cacciata*, literally "to hunt the hunted". In any hunting games, I know that I'd rather be the hunter than the ill-starred fox!

In this simple game the enjoyment is diminished if the "seek" is not sufficiently protracted. The "seek" is what reveals the "hide". The point is not so much finding the prey: on the contrary, the point is *not* finding it – that is, searching for it. The longer we search, the more meaningful the game.

Therefore, if we have been hiding from the Self with great talent and dedication, let us now seek the Self in a meaningful way. What matters most here is not necessarily *what* we find, but *how* we dedicate ourselves to finding it, and what we receive or learn from this dedication.

CHAPTER 6
HIDDEN CHAMBERS

Since 2015 there has been much controversy in Egyptian archaeology surrounding the tomb of Tutankhamun. Could there be another tomb hidden behind that of the great Pharaoh? Until recently, it was suspected that there might be hidden chambers there, and one theory was that one of these might be the last home of Queen Nefertiti, also believed by most to be the Pharaoh's stepmother.

If the prospect of finding the famous Queen's tomb, some 33 centuries after her burial, still seems plausible, how could we doubt our ability to locate our own contemporaneous Self? Our mission may not use radar scans, yet we will still need to probe deeply to explore those chambers where the Self may conceal itself.

For this phase of our exploration, we will look at the decision-making process as a series of interconnected rooms, within what we will call the COSARC Pyramid – to stay true to our archaeological metaphor. COSARC is not a royal city on the shores of the Nile but merely an acronym that might make this sequence a little more memorable.

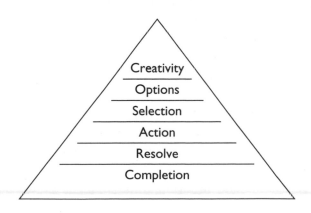

1 Creativity

"She did not know that imagination is the beginning of creation.
You imagine what you desire; you will what you imagine; and at last
you create what you will."

George Bernard Shaw

One issue I have with most books on decision making is the widespread view that one should start with a consideration of the options at hand. Although this seems highly logical, it is also true that logic can considerably limit our scope.

At a friend's birthday party recently, I met an affable young German, whose girlfriend was poking fun at him for his alleged lack of fantasy – to which he replied, "I am German, I use logic!"

I'm sure many German thinkers, such as Leibnitz, would have applauded. In fact, even a French philosopher, René Descartes, would have approved, only to be rebuffed, 150 years later, by another German thinker, Immanuel Kant.

In his *Critique of Pure Reason,* Kant questions many established rationalist wisdoms. "How is pure mathematics even possible?" he asks.

Kant believed that his new perspective was as revolutionary as Copernicus's theory of the movement of celestial bodies. Copernicus had turned astronomy inside out by giving a prime role to the position of the observer. He rejected the idea that the apparent movement of the stars inheres in the stars themselves, instead regarding it as an aspect of the spectator's experience. Here is Kant drawing the comparison explicitly:

"This would be just like the first thoughts of Copernicus, who, when he did not make good progress in the explanation of the celestial motions if he assumed that the entire celestial host revolves around the observer, tried to see if he might not have greater success if he made the observer revolve and left the stars at rest."

Similarly, for Kant, knowledge does not emanate from the object alone, but from the individual who observes it. Asserting that we cannot know things as they are "in themselves" (*das Ding an sich*), he elevates the role of experience in the acquisition of knowledge. And this experience relies on human sensations and intuition (*Anschauung*). We do not "receive" knowledge, we are involved in its inception.

How should this view inform our approach to decision making? Well, the answer is: by analogy. If in a Kantian or Copernican spirit we look at decisions not as abstract objects, but as something that emanates from the individual who faces a choice, we move toward a more holistic view of life.

Although the idea that a decision emanates from an individual may seem self-evident, it is valuable in implying that the starting-point cannot be merely laying out available options on a cold, clean slate, or doing the standard analytical listing of pros and cons. Instead, decision making has to involve tapping into our intuition. We may never attain the perfect decision (the *thing-in-itself* of the decision is unknowable), but our exploration must begin with our own feelings, sensations and intuition about what is needed. In that respect, all decisions – and especially tough decisions – are a voyage of self-discovery. This may be the very reason why they are so challenging: every decision wants to open a window onto our souls, even though we are sometimes reluctant to allow that.

Almost two centuries after Kant, the concept of intuition would inspire another prominent thinker. Carl Jung wrote: "*Intuition* is concerned with time. The intuitive person is able to 'see round corners', to have hunches about things, and is more interested in the possibilities of things than in their present existence." Jung's intuition sheds light on what is feasible in the outer world, the crystallization of the "possibilities of things". Intuition is what enables creativity.

How can we optimize this phase of intuition and creativity in our own decision making? Picasso felt that children are our best guides to creativity. He once said: "Every child is an artist. The problem is how to remain an artist after he grows up."

ORIENTATION POINT

Creativity in decision making depends heavily on intuition. This can often be nourished if you try to think like a child again. As adults we form attachments to what we believe are sophisticated ways of thinking, but often these approaches are over-complex and sidestep our most direct and deeply felt responses. Recapturing a child's direct vision can be deeply liberating.

This is the very problem that Darya Zabelina and Michael Robinson have endeavoured to solve. Zabelina and Robinson are two neuropsychologists from North Dakota State University who have researched adult creativity. They discovered that the more an adult tries to think like a child, the more creative he or she becomes. As part of their research, they gave two groups of graduate students the same creativity tests to complete. However, one group was primed with an additional element to the brief: "You are 7 years old." In those tests, the pretend 7-year-olds delivered consistently higher levels of creativity.

I can already imagine the cynics and rationalists among my readers chuckling over the implications of this. No, I will not suggest that you dress up as Superman or Cinderella before making an important decision! However, there is a serious point behind this image of the child, and its relevance to decision making.

"The child is a uniting symbol and brings together the separated and dissociated parts of the personality, which again has to do with the quality of being naïve," writes the psychonanalyst Marie-Louise von Franz. "But most people do not dare do this because one exposes oneself too much."

I think this general lack of comfort about relying on our inner child's intuition can be partly explained by the confusion between intuition on the one hand and impulse on the other.

Whereas intuition, which is self-generated, gets activated when we are relaxed and our minds are clear, impulse is always based on an external trigger, and is something we may live to regret (for example, the urge to shop online and similar compulsions). It is much harder to regret an intuition or a feeling, because how we feel deep down is by definition always true.

Moreover, all through the Neo-classical period right up to the Romantic movement of the 19th century there is an image of inspiration, according to which the artist is touched by divine breath. This is a notion we also find in antiquity, in Latin literature. Cicero, in his *Oration to the Poet Archias*, already refers to this idea in connection with the poet's inspiration as early as the 1st century BC. This is also reminiscent of the ancient and mystical Tree of Life, in Kabbalistic thinking and elsewhere.

The tree represents the spiritual path of ascent by humankind, as well as the descending path travelled by divine light (or the divine breath of inspiration) to reach the human being, God's creation. Light does not fall vertically from God to man: it follows a zigzagging ascent/descent movement through 10 spiritual principles and 22 paths.

This vertical and zigzagging ascent/descent is symbolically instructive of how we should handle inspiration – not as a force that is so remote and abstract that we will never access it; not as a divine exhalation so powerful that we could not possibly be equipped or worthy enough to receive it; but as an energy field which, if channelled properly, will enrich us immeasurably.

ORIENTATION POINT

The Tree of Life, in the mystic tradition known as Kabbalism, offers a zigzagging pattern for inspiration. This pattern is perfectly coherent. It evokes the idea that intuition favours the balanced, grounded soul whose life and all its dimensions — spiritual, physical, intellectual, social — are held in equilibrium.

---

2 Options

One of the key principles of negotiation, whether in diplomacy or in business (or even at home!), is that the more options we create (within reason), the more likely we are to arrive at a mutually satisfactory outcome.

Sometimes, people live under the illusion that they have no possibilities left, whether in a given situation or in their lives more broadly. "I've run out of options" is something you might hear them say.

In truth, we never really run out of options. Any situation is a junction from which many possibilities lead, even if some of them are hidden. It may seem that you face a stark choice: A or B. But close and creative inspection will often reveal A1, A2, A3 and so on, and perhaps even C, D, E and F. It depends on how you look at things — the Kantian emphasis again.

When we feel stuck, we could ask others what they would do in the same situation — especially if they have faced a similar scenario in the past. Their insights can be truly enlightening, not because of their complexity, but more often than not because of their surprising simplicity. In business, as in other fields, good decision making is often based on researching the precedents and using one's imagination to extract the relevant lessons.

Jung expressed the view that most neuroses reflect a form of psychological one-sidedness. If we can spot, even occasionally, the minutest seeds of anxiety or neuroticism in our difficulties with decision making, we should consider whether the root cause may not be a one-sided apprehension of things. Apprehension, of course, can mean either grasping something or fearing something — and probably both at the same time for many of us!

Studying other people's experiences gives us a multi-sidedness that can enrich our decision making and our lives. However, we should also aim to generate this multi-sidedness within ourselves, and by ourselves.

One way of achieving this is by *reframing* our decisions. An illustration of this would be the role played by US President Jimmy Carter in the resolution of the conflict between Egypt and Israel in the 1970s. Carter started losing hope that there would ever be peace between these two warring nations, as both were making strict demands on control of the Sinai desert, which Israel had conquered from Egypt during the Six-Day War in 1967.

Carter asked both parties why they insisted on this condition. For the Egyptian President Anwar Sadat it was a matter of national pride: Sinai had belonged to Egypt since the days of the Pharaohs; whereas for Israel's Prime Minister Menachem Begin it was a crucial matter of national security: having been attacked by Egypt on five occasions since 1948, the year of its declaration of independence, he felt his country urgently needed this "buffer zone" to protect itself.

The Camp David meetings started on 6 September 1978. The following day, Mrs Carter, the US President's wife, recorded the following:

"When the meeting was over at 1:30, Jimmy dictated his notes about the session [...]. I sat in. He said the meeting was mean. I had heard raised voices from the bedroom where I was working. They were brutal with each other, personal, and he had had to break into arguments at certain points. He said that he made notes, looking down at his pad so they would have to talk with each other instead of to him. Sometimes when their words became too heated he had to break in."

As negotiations kept hitting a wall, on 12 September Jimmy Carter "decided to work that afternoon on the terms for an Egyptian-Israeli treaty, and spread the Sinai maps out on the dining table to begin this task, writing the proposed agreement on a yellow scratch pad."

Carter asked Sadat to consider if he would be prepared to *regain sovereignty* over the Sinai desert, under the condition that it became a demilitarized zone. Begin was asked the reverse question: would he accept a *demilitarized Sinai*, under the condition that sovereignty were handed back to Egypt.

The rest is history. The Egyptian-Israeli Peace Treaty was signed on 26 March 1979, with a grand ceremony on the South Lawn of the White House, marking one of the most *decisive* geopolitical moves in the Middle East ever achieved.

This story illustrates the power of "reframing", and in particular how it can make the difference between deal or no deal, decision or no decision.

Reframing is such a powerful ploy that even when it does not alter the options, just rephrases them strategically, it can have a critical impact on our decisions. In Tversky and Kahneman's research on the framing of decisions, subjects were asked whether they would opt for surgery if the survival rate were 90 per cent, while others were told that the mortality rate was 10 per cent. The first framing increased acceptance, even though the situation remained identical.

The need for creativity, the generation of multiple options, the importance of framing (with the preference given to "interests" over "positions") – a repertoire of negotiation techniques is beginning to form, all of them having strong parallels with decision making, because fundamentally decisions are an intimate negotiation we engage in – with ourselves.

Moreover, just like a negotiation, a decision is often about respecting timing, and using silence. It is also about respecting the other party – the other part of ourselves – and, in this inner dialogue, not using disparaging language ("you are not qualified to make a decision," "you know nothing about this subject," "you are awful at making decisions").

To echo yet another concept from the field of negotiation, decision making is also about avoiding a single-issue focus. I had this experience when I bought my first apartment in London. As for most people, the limiting factor was budget. One day, immediately after visiting a property and experiencing yet another disappointment, the estate agent told me that he had just signed up a new property in the same neighbourhood. If the owner, a charming old lady, was there, she probably wouldn't object to my seeing the place ahead of the flat being advertised.

Naturally, I agreed on the spot, and upon viewing the residence immediately fell in love with it. My offer at the asking price was accepted, and we exchanged contracts a few weeks later. Finally, on the night before completion (the final and mutually binding signature of contracts), I received an email from the charming old lady, apologising for a sudden change of mind: she had decided to pull the property from the market. Needless to say, the way I felt was somewhere between devastation and anger, and I was in the process of emailing her a very unambiguous piece of my mind, when I decided to "press pause". I had realized that for someone who teaches negotiation, I was probably missing a trick!

Therefore, I reflected on this notion of single-variable negotiations. Was there another variable I could have missed? In the second iteration of my email, I wrote about my disappointment, but also my understanding that she could not have made this decision lightly. The only favour I was asking from her was to shed some light on the motivation behind her sudden U-turn. Was it about price? (Property values were rising at this time.) After a few hours she replied, thanking me for taking it so well (if only she knew!). She explained that she was still happy with the terms of the deal we had struck. Her main concern, however, was that the time from first viewing to completion had been so condensed that she had not been able to find a new property and was reluctant to enter into a rental agreement. What she was making clear to me was that there was another essential variable: timing.

In my reply, I did not increase my bid, but offered to finalize the acquisition while letting her stay in the flat for anything up to an additional three months, at no cost to her, to give her more time to find her own dream property. She accepted my offer, we completed on the same day, and she found a new place, only a few weeks later.

The relevance of this anecdote is that when facing tough decisions, not only do we need to create more options, we also need to establish what the main variables are, and to question ourselves regarding our underlying motivations. This too is about interests, not positions.

And let us remember that we always negotiate with (ideally not against) a counterpart. And the more we know about them, the more likely we are to reach an agreement.

Therefore, we need to ask ourselves these questions: which parts of me are involved in this inner negotiation and what does each part of me want? Once we have established these points, we must try to figure out what are our "must haves" versus our "nice to haves". (Psychotherapist Petruska Clarkson, in her work on couples therapy, advises that we should list our "must haves", our "nice to haves", as well as our "happy to let you haves" when selecting a partner – a particularly important decision!)

Once we have come to our conclusions, we shall be prepared for our negotiation – which is a powerful metaphor for our decisions. The need to consider multiple variables, the importance of listening to the other person, as well as creativity and reframing – these are all key considerations for negotiators, and therefore key considerations for the negotiations with ourselves that our decisions represent.

"Give me six hours to chop down a tree and I will spend the first four sharpening the axe."

It is telling that this quote has long been – albeit wrongly – attributed to Abraham Lincoln, against the evidence that (a) it never really takes six hours to chop down a tree, and (b) the earliest known publication of the remark dates back to 1956, almost a century later than the alleged presidential tree felling. But this apocryphal attribution probably says a lot about its natural authority and appeal.

Similarly, if decisions are about wielding the axe of separation, then we too need to invest time in sharpening it.

3 Selection

"When making a decision of minor importance, I have always found it advantageous to consider all the pros and cons. In vital matters, however, such as the choice of a mate or profession, the decision should come from the unconscious, from somewhere within ourselves. In the important decisions of personal life, we should be governed, I think, by the deep inner needs of our nature."

These are the words of Sigmund Freud, the father of psychoanalysis. His dual approach to decision making has echoes in the modern age in the research done by Daniel Kahneman and featured in his book *Thinking, Fast and Slow*. Here Kahneman describes two different ways in which thoughts are formed in the brain: "System 1" is fast, automatic and subconscious; "System 2" is slow, logical and conscious.

A few years ago this view was challenged by a team from Radboud University Nijmegen in The Netherlands. In their controversial opinion, there also exists a third mode of thought formation ("System 3") to account for decisions that are important and may require a more prolonged time for consideration, but use unconscious thinking rather than just logic to come to a decision. These include, for example, decisions surrounding creative or scientific problem solving or major life changes – what Freud called "vital matters". For those decisions, researchers believe that System 2, the slow and considerate mode, may even be harmful. Dijksterhuis writes, in reference to artistic creativity: "If you try to verbalize information when a decision should be largely based on non-verbalizable information, decisions suffer from conscious deliberation."

We also find a three-tier model of decision making in Steve Peters' *Chimp Paradox*. He describes the three systems rather more graphically as follows:

- *The Chimp*, whose agenda is primitive, motivated by its instinct for procreation and survival. Its defining mode is impulsive behaviour without concern for the consequences – it is driven, instead, by emotion.
- *The Human*, who is compelled by a social agenda and, in contrast to the chimp, is concerned with the consequences of its actions. Its mode of thinking is rational.
- *The Computer*, which is the part of our psyche that we (either as chimp or human) have trained to deal with apparently repetitive scenarios. Additionally, the Computer plays a part in predicting outcomes.

Despite the similarities between the above models, there are just as many differences between them. As these are only *models* of decision making, they will be at best an instructive approximation of how we actually decide. However, the fact that these three accounts do not tell exactly the same story does not mean that any of them should be dismissed outright.

We all know how models can be both instructive and misleading. A perfect example is Jung's modelization of "psychological types" as Thinking-, Feeling-, Sensation- or Intuition- based. Although this served a purpose at the time, it is now broadly believed to be a narrow interpretation of the human range of personalities. In psychoanalyst Anthony Storr's words, "I think it is fair to say that this [...] classification is one of Jung's least satisfactory contributions."

So, if psychology only gets us so far, we may need to use different tools from our archaeologists' kit to pursue our exploration from here. In fact, we need to return to our old favourite: etymology.

"Selection" is a rich word from an etymological point of view. Please bear with me now whilst I perform a few linguistic excavations.

"Selection" comes from the Latin *selectus*, meaning "chosen" but also "culled". It is made up of the prefix *se-*, which we find in words like "secret" to indicate that we set something aside; and of *lectus*, from *legere* meaning to gather, which we find in "lecture", a gathering of words.

Now we get to the heart of the matter. The word "selection" contains the notion of a two-way movement: we first gather things which are similar (*legere*) in order to then remove one from the lot (prefix *se-*).

In decision making, the option that was removed from the lot and taken aside also ends up being culled, sacrificed. It has been abducted from the multi-colour world of possibility and thrown into the black-and-white world of contingency.

This is the "cutting off" at the heart of the word "decision", something we already referred to in the Introduction (see page 7).

So where do we find the strength to perform this act? The answer is: in discernment. This is the quality we need at this crucial time. It is also the quality that ensures that, when on the battlefield (whether real or metaphorical), we fully participate yet remain unscathed. Discernment can be our greatest armour.

The French language has the perfect phrase for discernment: *faire la part des choses*. To my knowledge no precise translation of this phrase is possible. The closest expression in English may be "to separate the wheat from the chaff", but there is something worth exploring in the French formulation: it literally means to allocate to each thing its due. This implies that decisions made with discernment are – by nature – equitable. What this also means, as we know from decades of cognitive science and psychoanalytical theory, is that such decisions are cleansed of the influence of biases, and made with high consciousness, rather than by our "fake selves".

This notion of equity does not have a moral dimension: this is about equity between ideas, abstract entities, not between people. However, we are still looking at equity as a virtue.

Virtue for the ancient Greeks is closely linked with the notion of excellence. For example, a person displays virtue in their profession if he or she performs their work to the highest standard. The virtue of a human being or even of an object rests in their ability to perform, in the best possible way, the role they are intended to play.

Aristotle's definition of virtue is "a disposition to behave as a mean between extremes of deficiency and excess". For example, a coward will suffer disproportionate fear in the face of a difficult decision, whereas a person who is reckless is insufficiently wary, and may even seek the thrill of fear we described earlier.

Implied in this definition is the idea that each virtue has not one opposite, but two. The opposite of courage is both cowardice and recklessness. For Aristotle, we achieve virtue by finding a middle ground, not by aiming for an extreme. Virtue is therefore about moderation.

It follows that discernment itself is about finding the middle way between two extremes – rather than the one elusive option that would maximize our objectives. This does not constitute a preference for compromise or, worse, for mediocrity. On the contrary, it means that every challenging decision calls upon us to find the right central position between the two most radical outcomes we could aim for.

Imagine, for example, you are contacted by a headhunter to join a competitor, in a more senior position. You feel loyal to your current company, but at the same time are attracted by the prospect of promotion. This dilemma can make your decision challenging. What virtue means in this context is finding a position that allows you to honour the sense of loyalty to your current firm whilst allowing yourself to receive the promotion you feel you deserve. Giving your current company a chance to make a counter-offer would be a way to serve both aspirations.

ORIENTATION POINT

Decision making is about discernment – including discerning what your personal needs and priorities are. To focus too much on the details of the possible choices that appear to be available can lead to a decision that is not thoroughly informed by self-knowledge – and therefore flawed. Think of yourself as steering a ship through a complicated passage amidst hazards. Your ultimate concern is not the hazards but the ship itself, which must end up (a) intact, safe, and (b) set toward an appropriate future.

The most difficult decisions tend to involve two or more conflicting aspirations. For example, let's say I want to take a ten-month sabbatical from my regular work to write my next book. Here, I will be faced with two opposite dispositions of the mind:

- *One inner message tells me:* Follow your calling and take as much time off as you need to complete the book.
- *Another inner message tells me:* Think about your work, your commitment to your company and your colleagues. Surely, you can find enough time during holidays and weekends to do your writing.

The mean between the two cannot always be arrived at easily, like a simple arithmetic average. It is whatever happens when I position my soul in between the two dispositions. It may then turn out that asking for a six-month sabbatical is what will make me feel that I respect equally my calling to write my next book *and* my commitment to the firm and to my colleagues.

Aristotle used the word *hexis* to denote virtue. *Hexis* is not, for Aristotle, something that we happen to be gifted with or not: it is an active state, something we enact for ourselves. We are at the epicentre of what makes an action virtuous, in that it is our duty to maintain a stable equilibrium of the soul. Ultimately, it is our practice of, and familiarity with, this equilibrium of the soul that builds up our consciousness and our character.

Our consciousness is at the heart of discernment, which is not so much about "what?", but essentially about "who?" It is less about the decision's "variables" than the position of the person deciding: have they navigated the arduous passage through the extremes of possibility and, as a result of this regular practice, perfected their discernment?

Taking this thought further, we come to the conclusion that discerning between options should come second to discerning between the parts of ourselves that want something, and finding the ideal mean between them.

No decision can be deemed fully virtuous (and therefore "excellent") without this knowledge, even when, through the random operation of good luck, it leads to a positive result. In many ways, this could be the least instructive and the most misleading outcome.

4 Action

"Action!" We all know the associations of this word, as shouted by film directors from Pinewood to Hollywood – and Bollywood! Sometimes a director will allow the actors to improvise, but such liberties always take place within carefully chosen parameters. Most directors will plan every detail of the sequence to be "shot" (could this be the moment when the culling happens?).

With "Action!", we shift from one time zone to the next – from *kairos* to *chronos* (see page 45). The sequence to be filmed during the "action" phase will happen in real time. And because nothing can get in the way, doubt is not welcome to the party – it would only lead to postponing.

In *Measure for Measure*, Shakespeare wrote: "Our doubts are traitors, and make us lose the good we oft might win by fearing to attempt." Voltaire offers a contrasting perspective: "Doubt is not a pleasant condition, but certainty is absurd." I would agree only insofar as apparent certainties may turn out to be prejudices in disguise.

My view is that when we get to "action", there should be no room left for the *expression* of doubt. Doubt may have a home in the previous three rooms of Creativity, Options and Selection, but Action could be defined as the dynamic that follows the silencing of any doubts. They may still exist, but they had every opportunity to be entertained in the previous three chambers. At this stage, allowing doubt into the room would derail action, and send us back, together with our doubts, to the place where we started. Doubt would then be invested with a toxic aura, undermining our inner negotiations.

So, what does it take to silence doubt and create this positive dynamic? How can we take the dive into the deep – the leap of faith?

Cyrille is one of my childhood friends. Born three months apart, we have been friends all our lives. He miraculously came through a life-threatening illness and was transformed by the experience. If he now seems somewhat more detached from the world around him, he has also gained in insight and serenity in an inspiring way. I remember his words during one of our recent 12-legged walks (two humans and two dogs): "The world wasn't made by people who doubt." I find that there is so much truth in this. And similarly, our individual world will not be born out of the parts of us that doubt.

Of course, taking the necessary leap of faith is not easy. We've all been there before, standing on the diving board, staring at the pool below … and feeling the courage leaking out of us, drop by drop, with every second that passes.

But then, how did we learn to dive as children? Answer: by diving. We learn to ride by riding (and occasionally falling from a bike or a horse), we learn to act by acting, we learn public speaking by speaking in public; and so we must learn to decide by deciding.

Nonetheless, there will always be fear. Nothing great was ever achieved without an element of nerves. Cicero wrote in his *De Oratore* that the public speaker who doesn't feel nervous before delivering a speech will do a wretched job!

Part I of this book was all about those fears. This is one moment in our exploration when they come back to haunt us: immediately before and immediately after we say in our minds the word "Action!"

Any of the seven fears of decision making may do a reprise performance at this point: the fear of making the wrong choice, of missing out, failing, reaching new heights, identification, lack of recognition, or selfishness.

Any of these has the power to unravel, layer by layer, all the good work we have accomplished together until this moment.

We established, in Part I, that these fears, unless properly managed, lead us to build unhelpful defence mechanisms. We also traced them back to the "yearning to return". *Each decision we make* takes us a step further from our mythical Eden, our remembered comfort.

Clearly, it doesn't help that humankind's first recorded decision, back in the Garden, is the Original Sin – not the best start to a life of independent decision making! Or could it be just that? It is, after all, our founding act as decision-making humans. This led Schopenhauer to regard our original sin as our original design: "The great truth that really constitutes the heart of Christianity is the doctrine of original sin (affirmation of the will) and redemption (denial of the will); whereas everything else is mostly only wrapping and covering, or simply accessories."

The fact is that the Original Sin, through breaching the tacit contract with God, marks the start of our lives outside the Garden, even if it comes with the yearning to return (not to mention the need to earn a living!).

There are other passages in the Bible too where someone is expelled from home. Take the story of Abraham. The parallel with the previous story is that if Adam is the first man, Abraham is the first Hebrew – the founder of a nation and a faith.

God said to Abram (Abraham's name before he is tasked by God with the creation of the Hebrew nation): "Go out from your country, from your birthplace, from the home of your father, to the land which I will show you ..." (Genesis 12.1). This is the passage where God commands Abram to leave his father's house to travel to Canaan. The instruction in Hebrew is "*Lekh-Lekha*". The usual translation is "Go out" (from your country and your father's house), but in fact this expression has a dual meaning: it can also be translated as "Go toward yourself."

The word "going" (*Lekh*) has the connotation in the Bible "of moving toward one's ultimate purpose, toward your soul's essence, that for which you were created".

So, the act of leaving one's intimate comfort zone, whether Eden for Adam, or the family home and birthplace for Abraham, is also the journey that takes us to ourselves, our true essence and our ultimate purpose.

If the yearning to return is regressive, the opposite, progressive path, is the one that will take us away from the Garden, toward growth and fulfilment. We need to be dead to Eden – or for Eden to die in us – in order to be able to grow.

Life outside Eden involves accepting responsibility for our actions, rather than being immobilized by guilt or shame.

This way of looking at life makes the greatest difference between fate and destiny. Fate is something that happens to us, but remains "outside us" – hence we feel we have no control. But this absence of control is not the only reason we suffer from the effects of fate: it may well be that we were just not present. As Carl Jung wrote, "when an inner situation is not made conscious, it happens outside, as fate."

Destiny is fate plus presence, or fate plus consciousness. Some might argue the difference is that fate is all down to luck, or lack of it. However, I believe even luck follows the same pattern. We make our luck the same way we make our destiny. We may not have all the cards, but if we have a good enough hand, this may be all we need.

I was once feeling sorry for someone who had been particularly unlucky in life, and I was expressing this feeling to a friend's mother, Helene Leneman, once a well-known art gallerist in Paris. Helene was a lady of great culture, a friend of Marc Chagall and other great artists from the Paris School. She had spent her youth in Eastern Europe, where she had helped many orphaned children find a home and start a new life after the Second World War. She knew a thing or two about luck.

She said to me: "The Hebrew word for luck is *mazal*, and the three consonants that make up this word – *Mem* ("M"), *Zain* ("Z") and *Lamed* ("L") – are the first letters of the words meaning Place, Time and Learning."

According to the ancient sages, luck is the convergence – as if our stars were aligned (the etymology of *mazal* is linked to the stars) – of being in the right place, at the right moment, equipped with the right knowledge. And it is clear we have some responsibility for, or at least some influence over, all three dimensions.

The same is true of our decisions: we may not be able to control their outcomes, but we can influence when, where and with what preparation and knowledge we face them. The alternative is indecisiveness, which is a belief in, and an admission of, our powerlessness.

James Hollis wrote about another form of powerlessness, that which affects children of abusive parents, and how they often end up themselves getting married to abusive partners. His explanation is that "The depth of the programmed powerlessness is greater than the hurt of the abuse."

In many ways, the same can be said of indecisiveness. The depth of our programmed indecisiveness, through either the examples set by our parents, or our own experiences, can be greater than the hurt of procrastination. Hollis writes that, in the case of abuse, we enter collusion with powerlessness. Turning to the analogous realm of decision making, this is exactly what we want to avoid: colluding with indecisiveness.

Although we may be agnostic on the question of religion, there is one form of agnosticism we cannot allow ourselves. If the "action" phase of decisions involves the leap of faith discussed earlier, it needs to start with faith in ourselves: the belief that we can do it. Agnostics and believers have something major in common: they can neither prove – nor disprove – the existence of God. The only difference between them is faith. If we keep disrupting our decisions, hindering our actions with doubt, losing the faith we need to make the necessary jump, we also lose faith in our decision-making ability, and ultimately in ourselves: we become self-agnostic.

5 Resolve

The previous chamber in our COSARC pyramid was Action: acting upon our choices, the moment of separation between the worlds of possibility and contingency. If action is that moment, a decision is nothing without duration, without our being loyal to our intention for the time required to transform an action from idea into reality.

Some people would refer to "Action" as the decision. But what would be the point of a decision devoid of this essential phase? What would be the value of a choice that may be enacted but not monitored throughout its realization, with no one seeing it through to its consequences?

"Resolve" is also the opposite of a behaviour commonly known as "buyer's regret". Statistics from SDC, a professional retail organization, tell us that 8 to 9 per cent of goods purchased at stores will be returned, and that 25 to 30 per cent of e-retail orders will be sent back. It seems that indecisiveness is a common phenomenon indeed.

However, I think that buyer's regret, and more broadly, the lack of resolve, not only highlight a weakness in our moment of choice ("Action"): they also reveal potential weaknesses throughout the decision-making pyramid. We receive a critical clue that the Self may be hiding, or stuck, in one of the previous four chambers, and that we need to question ourselves to locate it and re-engage with it. Did we use enough creativity? Did we generate enough options? Did we select an option that truly suits us? Did we act positively and hopefully?

The origin of the verb to *resolve* is instructive. It is only from the 16th century that the word comes to mean to decide, to determine. In the 15th century, *resolve* means to separate into different parts – an application that has remained in use in optics to this day. Going back in time, up to the 14th century, *resolve* means to melt, to dissolve, to reduce to liquid.

Whether metaphorically or not, this points to an alchemical notion: the process of separating elements and melting them together to create a new entity.

What does this have to do with decision making? The answer can be found in Martin Buber's *The Way of Man*, whose third chapter is called "Resolution" – a variation on our present theme.

Buber warns us of something that hinders us from achieving our purpose: that is, the "patchwork" way in which we may approach a task, with "the advance and subsequent retreat; it is the wavering, shilly-shallying character [...] that makes it questionable. The opposite of 'patchwork' is work 'all of a piece'." Now, how does one achieve work "all of a piece"? Only with a united soul, answers Buber.

The philosopher's point is that it is in a person's power to unify his or her soul, and "pull himself together".

Buber describes this unification as a continuous process. Any work done with the unified soul reacts on the soul and leads to greater unification. By all manner of detours we progress to steadier unity. In other words, to put the matter more simply, good decision making is self-perpetuating.

In another passage, Buber relates the moment when a highly respected teacher surprises his students playing a game of checkers. "Do you know the rules of checkers?" he asks. And when out of shyness they do not reply, he himself gives the answer: "I shall tell you the rules of checkers. The first is that one must not make two moves at once. The second is that one may only move forward and not backward. And the third is that when one has reached the last row, one may move wherever one likes."

The word used by Buber, translated into English as "resolution", is *Entschlossenheit*. There is something very definitive-sounding about this: it resonates with words like *geschlossen* ("closed") and *Schloss* ("castle"), conjuring images of unassailable medieval fortresses. This is the term also used by Martin Heidegger to mean something more specific than *resolution*, namely: the state of being determined, or the state of being resolved.

Resolution is not just a phase in decision making. It is also a state of mind, even a state of being, a state of soul. On this note, we need to recognize that the temptation to go backward is ever present. We saw it previously in the "yearning to return", the elusive quest for a lost paradise. Unable to recapture our lost territory, we may end up recreating Eden elsewhere – perhaps in a region, a house, a job, a partner, even a habit.

Our journey toward decision making will encounter doubt along the way – indeed, it may even *be filled* with doubt. We may find ourselves surrounded by desert, a desolate and depressing wilderness where we had hoped for paradise regained. Pondering this, I'm reminded of something I once heard from the author and psychotherapist Martin Lloyd-Elliott: "the opposite of depression is expression." *Expression* will be the first step toward escaping from the desert. It can mean bouncing ideas with friends, with experts, or simply – and more usually – having an honest inner conversation, which will unveil those areas where the Self is hiding, and help us re-engage with our journey wholeheartedly.

Two and a half millennia ago, Confucius said: "Wheresoever you go, go with all your heart". What Buber does is to break this down into separate instructions: go one step at a time and don't ever go backwards; when you eventually get there, you will find no limit to where you can go.

6 Completion

Our search for the Self in the six chambers of the COSARC pyramid comes to a natural conclusion here.

Could it be that the Self occasionally hides in this "completion chamber"? This would apply to a situation where we successfully create or identify options, select our favoured one, and even act upon it and monitor its implementation – until, finally, we find ourselves unable to let go and move on. This could be because our work is finished, and we are unable to detach ourselves from it; or because it is "almost" finished and we seek perfection; or because we realize it will never be finished.

In a recent interview, Pinin Brambilla Barcilon, the artist who for 20 years conducted the restoration of Leonardo's *Last Supper* mural in Milan, explained that she experienced serious withdrawal symptoms upon completing her work. This was despite the pressure from her husband and children, who felt she had neglected them during these two decades.

ORIENTATION POINT

Failing to recognize that something they had underway has now ended is an issue many people commonly face in daily life. A high level of mental and emotional engagement can continue even when that "something" has been problematic and stressful. You should be relieved at having, at last, a blank canvas again on which to work, but instead you are still working with hindsight on a finished piece within your portfolio. Your mental and emotional landscape is still, needlessly, cluttered. To clean the slate for effective decision making you need to recognize when an issue is concluded, for better or worse.

In business, people rarely have the luxury of enough time to seek perfection – for example, when launching a new product. Of course, they need to make sure their new product will meet all the necessary technical requirements (for example, complying with safety regulations); but by seeking constant improvement, they risk losing their "first mover" advantage, and letting a competitor reap the rewards of their hard work.

Another example from the business world comes from one of my clients, the investment management arm of a large insurer. This company had spent years working on the "perfect" strategy. I don't think their work on the new five-year strategy could be faulted. However, it took them so long to perfect and announce their plan that some key employees started worrying or losing faith, and made their own plans to leave before the new strategy went live.

So how does anyone ever decide that their work is done?

At the Gerhard Richter retrospective exhibition at London's Tate Modern gallery, I remember watching a filmed interview with the German artist, who was asked by Sir Nicholas Serota, the Gallery's Director, how he knew when a large abstract painting was finished. "When nothing disturbs me," Richter replied, "and I have no idea what to do more – but what I could add would destroy it. […] And suddenly it's finished."

For Richter, a great artist, the moment when a work of art is finished is unpredictable. It is not defined by a vision of the finished work. Instead, Richter relies on emotion, insight, to judge the point when further improvement would be destructive.

As with virtue, which as you will remember is a synonym for excellence in ancient Greece (see page 83), there is no peak of perfection, only a perfect balance between two extremes. For Richter, this balance means being on the cusp, treading a fine line, like an acrobat, between just enough and too much. As we get closer to completing a work (or making a decision), this dividing line becomes thinner: it is only when we intuitively know, at the last moment, that the next brush stroke on the canvas will worsen the result that our work can be deemed complete.

Devil in the details

Having embarked on our quest for the Self, we have now explored all the rooms where it can reside and conceal itself. This amounts to one possible version of immobility – the Self finding a refuge in one of the six chambers of the pyramid. There is, however, another source of immobility. In this case, the Self is not hiding in the chambers themselves: rather, it is to be found somewhere *between* chambers, not necessarily because it is hiding but potentially because it is stuck, in the antechambers or at the junction between chambers, or maybe at the hinges of the doors. The word for "hinge" in French is *charnière*, and its etymology is the Latin *cardo* meaning "essential point", or "cardinal point".

We should not dismiss the hinges as inconsequential: this could be the most crucial location for the Self, the place where we are most likely to find it.

In order to find the Self, we need to question its alibis. Why should it be stuck? I can think of three reasons:

1 Take-overs

This is what happens when the reason we give for not deciding is: "I'm not even sure I know what I want."

In this case, it feels we have abandoned our most primordial responsibility toward ourselves, even before acting according to our will. We have, in fact, failed to identify our will. It feels like we have lost track, we may even have lost ownership – a daunting state in which all certainties dissolve.

> "I am all in a sea of wonders. I doubt. I fear. I think strange things, which I dare not confess to my own soul. God keep me, if only for the sake of those dear to me!"

These are the words of Jonathan Harker, the traveller in Bram Stoker's novel *Dracula*, upon his arrival at the castle of the long-caped, long-toothed Count.

Our will makes us human. Negating it, abandoning it, equates to giving in to a more powerful presence. In Bram Stoker's novel, this presence is a vampire. In our lives, it can be a person, a group of people, an institution, a fear.

I'm not going to recommend we hang a bunch of garlic outside our home, or resort to exorcism. However, I think the metaphor is vividly apt. Remember, in vampire stories, what happens to humans who stand in front of a mirror, next to a vampire. They can only see their own reflection: the vampire remains invisible, a mere vision of the mind. The risk is that if we succumb to that vision, if we make it our reality, our reflection will, in turn, disappear. The Self will have vacated its space.

Therefore, if we feel our will has been taken over, that we cannot identify what we want, we need to reclaim the Self, from whatever power, real or imaginary, holds it under its spell.

ORIENTATION POINT

Not having clear and firm priorities is an obvious disadvantage in decision making. So too is having priorities to which you merely give lip service, as if voicing them were enough, even if you lack the will to act upon them. You may even think you *believe* in a priority. But then when decision time comes, you may find yourself unable to carry it out, proving that it was illusory – and self-deluding – all along. *Inhabiting* your priorities, or allowing them wilful life as they inhabit you, is as important as knowing them.

2 The Ulysses Pact

This expression is used in medicine to describe a decision made freely in the present that binds us firmly in the future. It is applied to patients whose ability to make decisions in the future is likely to be compromised by ill health.

The origin of the idea is to be found in Homer's *Odyssey*, and specifically the episode in which Ulysses (or Odysseus) asks his crew to tie him to the mast, to preserve his life as the ship approaches the seductive Sirens, who are intent on luring him to his doom. He also, on the advice of the sorceress Circe, plugs his crew's ears with beeswax, to make sure they too are immune to the Sirens' enticing songs.

In our decisions we constantly encounter potential for distraction. It is reassuring to read, in Homer's poem, that after a ten-year journey Ulysses successfully returns to his wife Penelope in Ithaca. This is achieved only through his total dedication, despite the many occasions when this quality was tested.

In our everyday lives there are no physical masts to be tied to when we risk being distracted from our decisions. However, making a vow or formal commitment may be seen as a metaphorical version thereof. Our resolve should instead be something we gather within ourselves and harden.

3 The Comedian's Lesson

I listened once to a leading stand-up comedian (to my mind improvised stand-up comedy is one of the most challenging of all professions) who commented on the qualities required to succeed in his line of work. The trick is, essentially, he said, "to think fast, and for this, to relax one's grip". Stand-up improvisation is nothing if not the ability to *decide* on the spur of the moment – in this case, to decide on what is most likely to generate laughter and applause.

The attitude of relaxing one's grip is described by Carl Jung, in his commentary on *The Secret of the Golden Flower* (a classic Chinese Taoist meditation text), where he quotes a letter from a former patient:

"By keeping quiet, repressing nothing, remaining attentive, and by accepting reality – taking things as they are and not as I wanted them to be – by doing all this, unusual knowledge has come to me, and unusual powers as well, such as I could never have imagined before. I always thought that when we accepted things they overpowered us in some way or other. This turns out not to be true at all, and it is only by accepting them that one can assume an attitude toward them. So now I intend to play the game of life, being receptive to whatever comes to me, good and bad, sun and shadow for ever alternating, and, in this way, also accepting my own nature with its positive and negative sides. Thus, everything becomes more alive to me. What a fool I was! How I tried to force everything to go according to the way I thought I ought to!"

This passage eloquently outlines the benefits of relaxing one's grip. This is about accepting events, not fighting them. It is about being receptive to life around us and, as a result, sacrificing the ego's mundane goals and elevating ourselves to a higher rung on the ladder of the Self. This is the only way to make sure our Will is moving freely, rather than stuck in the same place.

***

Where do we currently stand in our journey? Well, in Part I we concluded by addressing the fears of the *implication* our decisions have *for the Self*, while in Part II we focused on the *implication of the Self* for our decisions. We then took part in a treasure hunt for the Self, wherever it may hide – looking in the six chambers of decision making, as well as the anti-chambers and even the door hinges. After such a thorough search, we have by now no doubt found the Self's likely location.

The last challenge that Part II has highlighted is the necessity for movement, for the dynamic of the Will across the six chambers, and for the need to relax our grip in order to enable the momentum of decision making to happen. This momentum is what we will explore in Part III.

KEY SKILL 3

HOW TO USE INTUITION

"… decision making has to involve tapping into our intuition."
(see page 75)

Intuition is a deeper source of insight than either instinct or rational thought. Instinct is our automatic emotional reaction to a situation – often an immediate experience of either attraction or revulsion. Rational thought is mental processing using the same structures that underlie language – including concepts such as "therefore", "instead" and "despite". Intuition is unique in being both wordless and profound. Its messages often seem to be projected from some inner oracle. They are based, in reality, on a hidden fund of self-awareness, experience and empathy.

The feel-right factor

Intuition is what tells us that something somehow does or does not *feel* right. In popular speech this might be termed the message of the heart rather than the head – since these two message-centres are commonly in conflict, pointing in opposite directions when it comes to decision making.

Relying on intuition can improve our decisions and enhance our confidence in making them. For example, imagine you have prepared a speech with a number of jokes in it, intended to lighten the tone and make your serious message more palatable. Once you enter the room, you become aware of a "vibe" that tells you you should drop the jokes. Somehow you are picking up on the mood of your audience, before they gather round you to listen. This is intuition, guiding you from a viewpoint supplied by years of empathy.

Experience is an important ingredient in intuition's chemistry. Your intuition is constantly growing, gathering into itself all the lessons you have learned unconsciously in all your years on the planet to date.

One advantage of intuition, compared with rational thought, is that it offers a shortcut to decision making, obviating the need to master mountains of data. This does not mean you should make your decisions blind, on the evidence of intuition alone. Instead, intuition allows you to practise the technique of "thin slicing" – using small data samples instead of sifting the huge amount of information theoretically available to you.

Light in the labyrinth

Faced with an important decision, any conscientious individual is likely to research thoroughly the evidence on all sides of the question. The human brain, though, does not have the processing capacity of a computer, and in any case much of the evidence will be ambivalent in the direction it points. That is why intuition is so useful. While you have been sifting the data, your "gut", as we often like to say, has been accumulating a whole archive of imperceptible signals, some positive, some negative. When it comes to decision making, the gut will then either confirm or deny the rational self's provisional choices. *All* choices should be seen as provisional subject to receiving the intuition's approval. If you feel a doubt materializing, attend to it closely. It may be fear, an habitual response based on long-established flaws in your self-image; or it may be intuition's wisdom, steering you in the right direction.

Optimum conditions

The following strategies are designed to make it more likely that intuition will serve you well in your decision making.

- *Allow yourself time*
  Intuition happens quickly but may take hours, days or weeks for you to process, depending on the situation. Do not force yourself into schedules that make it difficult for intuition to play its part in your decision making.
- *Find a quiet place*
  Pondering the situation in a quiet place, far from the action, makes it likelier that intuition will come up with the answers you seek. Be reflective. Do mindful deep breathing exercises, to keep any stress at bay.
- *Consult Morpheus*
  Morpheus is not a voice-activated virtual assistant but the Greek god of dreams. Getting a good night's sleep creates the perfect conditions for intuition to operate. The answer may not come to you in a dream but the next morning you will be more receptive to the inner voice's messages.

PART III
THE MOMENTUM
OF DECISIVENESS

CHAPTER 7

OF THE ESSENCE

"It is the same with people as it is with riding a bike. Only when moving can one comfortably maintain one's balance".

Albert Einstein, in a letter to his son Eduard, 1930

Why dedicate the penultimate part of this book to the Momentum of Decisiveness, rather than jump directly to the main object of our pursuit, the Deciding Mind and how we make our smartest decisions?

The answer is that in this book we are patiently moving one step at a time. We have uncovered the potential motivations not to make a decision, and the reasons why we might get stuck. Now we turn to look at the engine of decision making.

Momentum is what drives our choices across the six chambers of decision making through to their realization. How does this happen? And how can we favour the conditions of momentum?

This new stretch of the road is not without its own perils. These are not outside obstacles, such as another person's will: they are invisible inner obstacles, which only manifest themselves when momentum is reduced or absent.

Often a project might start well and engage us, but we find that we lose appetite later on, for no obvious reason. As a result, we become less interested in the work we have to do, and end up stalling it.

This is reminiscent of the story of Hannibal, the 3rd-century BC Carthaginian general, who dedicated his life to vanquishing the Roman Empire. Hannibal came very close to this objective following his victory in Cannae, one of the defining battles of the Second Punic War. One by one, several strongholds defected from Rome to Carthage. As the Roman historian Livy wrote, "How much more serious was the defeat of Cannae than those that preceded it can be seen by the behaviour of Rome's allies.

Before that fateful day, their loyalty remained unshaken. Now it began to waver for the simple reason that they despaired of Roman power."

At this stage, nothing seemed to stand in the way of Hannibal's eventual victory ... except for one important detail: momentum.

Instead of forging through to Rome and displaying the same resolve with which he had led his armies (complete with 37 elephants) first through Spain and Gaul, then through the Alps, and victoriously all the way to southern Italy, Hannibal decided to regroup in his newly established base at Capua before the final attack on Rome.

One of Hannibal's key generals urged him to march without delay toward Rome, but he rejected the advice. This interruption in the hitherto successful war momentum would prove to be the Carthaginians' undoing.

In popular culture this sojourn in Capua stands for the misjudged interruption of an effort, combined with unwarranted self-confidence – and also for a doomed indulgence in the good life. Capua fell back to the Romans, and Hannibal was recalled to Carthage to face more military defeats, which ultimately led to his voluntary exile.

The longevity of this story through two millennia is testimony to its eloquent illustration of the risks we face whenever we lose momentum.

Let us reflect on this word, *momentum*. It is concerned with speed, or more precisely, with velocity. (In physics, an object's momentum is its mass multiplied by its velocity.) How is velocity different from speed?

In everyday parlance, these terms are often understood as synonyms, yet their definitions differ in one major respect. Whereas speed is a *scalar* quantity, velocity is a *vector* quantity. Scalar quantities are represented by a magnitude (or numerical value) alone. Vector quantities are represented by both a magnitude and a direction. In other words:

$$\text{SPEED} = \frac{\text{DISTANCE}}{\text{TIME}}$$

$$\text{VELOCITY} = \frac{\text{DISPLACEMENT}}{\text{TIME}}$$

Let us imagine you were to fly from London to New York at a constant speed. This speed would be unaffected by the journey, irrespective of whether you flew in a straight line or decided to take a much longer route before eventually landing in New York.

In the case of velocity, what matters is displacement, not distance. In the above example, you may still be flying at a constant speed but your velocity would be dramatically reduced by opting for the longer route. The same displacement, the miles separating London from New York, would take much longer to travel. What this also implies is that if you left London and three hours after take-off were obliged to fly back there, your velocity would end up being zero, because your journey would end exactly where it started.

In a similar manner to velocity, momentum is a matter of the efficiency of the flow between our thoughts, leading to a decision. This is the flow between the six chambers of decision making. Momentum is concerned with the displacement from the need for a decision to the decision itself. Our ability to progress quickly through to the final chamber is irrelevant unless we have visited each chamber in turn. Similarly, our speed is irrelevant if we keep revisiting the same chambers, without being able to move on.

In other words, the speed at which we come to a decision is secondary to how seamlessly efficient is the flow toward that decision.

CHAPTER 8
DECISION FLOW

Now that we have explored the link between flow, speed and velocity, the next question becomes: how can we create and maintain our sense of flow and momentum?

Flow happens to be the title of a bestselling book by Mihaly Csíkszentmihályi, a Hungarian psychologist whose research establishes a link between flow and optimal performance, whether by an artist, a sportsperson, a scientist, a company CEO or anyone else. He defines flow as "being completely involved in an activity for its own sake. The ego falls away. Time flies. Every action, movement, and thought follows inevitably from the previous one, like playing jazz."

Flow is common to all human achievements, including our decisions. What can we learn from Csikszentmihalyi's research? And how does it help us achieve the kind of flow that is needed in decision making?

Creating flow

It is worth exploring some of the conditions behind the flow experience, focusing on their relevance to decision making.

Tasks we have a chance of completing

This could easily be misinterpreted as tasks that are *easy* to complete. What Csikszentmihalyi's research shows is that activities that are most likely to create flow are those that are challenging and at the same time require our most advanced skills.

This has been my experience when working with successful leaders: they are also people who do not get fazed by difficulty. On the contrary, they thrive on opportunities to exploit the greatest breadth of their skills in situations that are highly challenging and would defeat many others.

They tend to be much less engaged by "day-to-day" tasks, which they are only too happy to delegate.

Csikszentmihalyi explains that flow comes at a very specific point: "whenever the opportunities for action perceived by the individual are equal to his or her capabilities."

I believe this is a key reason why many procrastinators heighten the level of challenge posed by otherwise easy decisions, by postponing clusters of decisions until the very last minute. They may even admit they can only work well under pressure. What they may not realize is how often this pressure is entirely self-inflicted.

At the other end of the spectrum, doing low-challenge, low-skill tasks leads to apathy, boredom, worry and anxiety – the four horsemen of decision-apocalypse!

Paradox of control

Csikszentmihalyi shows that high achievers who live in flow share a commonality of approach, which has to do with their attitude regarding control.

People who experience flow do not seek to live in a risk-free world, or to control every element of risk. On the contrary they thrive under risk, knowing that the full use of their talent and skills will allow them to minimize that risk; and *potentially*, in the event of danger materializing, give them the confidence of being equipped to deal with it. Their experience is therefore about the *possibility* of control should the need arise, rather than the *actuality* of control at all times.

In any case, as Epictetus taught us almost two thousand years ago (see page 39), there is only so much we can control. Any attempt to override this limitation is doomed and will lead to the kind of fixation that results in *psychic entropy*, the opposite of flow.

For Csíkszentmihályi, it is only by relinquishing control over what is beyond our power that we can fully experience flow. Paradoxically, it is also how we can reach the kind of outcomes that our quest for control was trying to achieve in the first place.

The loss of self-consciousness

Flow happens when consciousness of the self is lost: the ego recedes into the background. As a result, flow experiences are largely egoless experiences. Csikszentmihalyi explains that the self that emerges from flow is stronger, more complex, having grown through the completion of a challenging task. Flow enriches the self by stretching us and expanding our skills.

He refers to the work of neurophysiologist Dr Jean Hamilton, who has established that "among people who reported flow frequently, activation decreased when they were concentrating. Instead of requiring more effort, investment of attention actually seemed to decrease mental effort [...]. This in turn suggests that people who can enjoy themselves in a variety of situations have the ability to screen out stimulation and to focus only on what they decide is relevant for the moment."

The opposite trait is "stimulus over-inclusion", a state in which our attention is easily distracted by irrelevant signals.

In addition to this, Csikszentmihalyi mentions two further personality profiles that prevent flow. One is excessive self-consciousness, which characterizes someone who is forever anxious about how others will perceive them and is afraid of creating a bad impression or of doing something inappropriate.

The other disqualifying personality profile appears when people are excessively self-centered. "A self-centered individual is usually not self-conscious, but instead evaluates every bit of information only in terms of how it relates to her desires [...]. Consciousness is structured entirely in terms of its own ends, and nothing is allowed to exist in it that does not conform to those ends."

The commonality between the above profiles lies in the use of psychic energy. Stimulus over-inclusion militates against flow because one's "psychic energy becomes too fluid and too erratic". Excessive self-consciousness and self-centeredness, on the other hand, prevent flow because one's attention has become too rigid, too narrowly focused.

People who experience flow dedicate themselves to "doing their best in all circumstances", but this does not mean pursuing the dictates of self-interest. Instead, it means committing to exerting their talents as effectively as possible to attain the optimum outcome.

As Csíkszentmihályi explains, they know they are not compelled to complete a task they have started, but something in them keeps them going and will not allow them to give in.

This is, I believe, both a source and a consequence of the flow experience.

Ultimately, if decision making requires the right momentum, understanding and nurturing flow helps us create this momentum and avoid any interruptions. If we live in fear that our decisions will change people's perception of us, or if we make decisions with a view to impressing them, we will certainly not achieve our best outcomes.

ORIENTATION POINT

Getting into the Zone, or the flow state, makes decisions more fluid
and organic. We seem to lose all sense of time, and it is almost as if our
consciousness were fused with its object of focus. The important point
here is that you do not have to *like* the subject matter of your decision
making to bring yourself into flow. What starts off as a burden can lead to
flow if you commit to it wholeheartedly.

CHAPTER 9
UNDER THE HOOD

At this stage of our exploration of Momentum, we have established the primacy of displacement over distance and, as a result, the significance of flow. Yet, flow itself is only the imprint of Momentum, the clearest signal that it is present. Flow does not create Momentum: rather, it is Momentum that generates flow. To grasp this point, it helps to think of a wind turbine. Contrary to what a child may think, it is not the turbine that generates wind: turbines need the wind to blow on their blades in order to generate power.

Hence the question: what happens when we open the hood, or bonnet, of the engine that is Momentum, and try to understand where, and how, flow is created inside?

To stay with this mechanical analogy, the first thing we notice when we do open the hood is the "drive belt", a critical part of the engine that distributes power to the rest of the vehicle.

Let us imagine that this drive belt is made up of two parts:

- The upper half, which is immediately visible when we open the bonnet of our vehicle.
- The lower half, which remains hidden until the engine is activated.

The Momentum "drive belt": upper half

The visible part of the belt is what we notice when we first open the hood. To move on from our metaphor, the hood of our Momentum has been opened many times by neuroscientists, among them Antonio Damasio, Head of the Department of Neurology at the University of Iowa College of Medicine.

Using electrodes or, in a much less invasive way, sophisticated image technology such as magnetic resonance scanning, neuroscientists are able to identify which parts of the brain are associated with specific thoughts, behaviours or emotions. The analysis of patients with brain damage gives unique insights into the relation between the affected part of the brain and the corresponding symptoms the patient is demonstrating.

Now, drawing upon such findings as well as upon a broader range of knowledge and experience, Damasio has shed valuable light on decision making, and in particular the way we tend to overemphasize the role of reason over emotions.

He gives the following examples of decisions that do not have a direct connection with reasoning:

- Our response to situations where our level of blood sugar drops, and neurons in the hypothalamus detect this decline. The ensuing hunger state, inciting us to eat, does not involve the use of conscious knowledge or reasoning.
- Our instinctive moving away from a falling object. Here again, our response does not use conscious knowledge or conscious reasoning. (However, we once had to learn consciously what our reaction should be in this situation, and this knowledge became engraved in our stimulus/response system, so that it happens automatically, without need for deliberation.)

Such reflections led Damasio to draw a distinction between the "high-reason" view of formal logic, valued by the likes of Plato and Descartes, and the "somatic-marker" view, whereby we pay attention primarily to physical impressions ("somatic markers"), such as our "gut feelings". Damasio asserts that "somatic markers may not be sufficient for normal human decision making since a subsequent process of reasoning and final selection will still take place in many though not all instances." Yet in the same passage he adds that "somatic markers probably increase the accuracy and efficiency of the decision process. Their absence reduces them."

In a later publication Damasio further explores the respective roles of reason and emotion in decision making. He tells the story of a 65-year-old woman with a long history of Parkinson's disease. Her condition no longer responded to levodopa, a chemical precursor of the neurotransmitter dopamine. He explains that "dopamine is missing in certain brain circuits of Parkinson's patients, much as insulin is missing in the bloodstream of patients with diabetes. [...] Unfortunately, the medications designed to increase dopamine in the brain circuits where it is missing do not help all patients."

An alternative form of treatment involves implanting small electrodes in the brain stem of Parkinson's patients. This approach delivers impressive results, as the symptoms seem to miraculously disappear.

This is what happened with this particular patient: the doctors found one electrode contact that greatly relieved her symptoms.

> "But the unexpected happened when the electric current passed through one of the four contact sites on the patient's left side, precisely two millimetres below the contact that improved her condition. The patient stopped her ongoing conversation quite abruptly, cast her eyes down and to her right side, then leaned slightly to the right and her emotional expression became one of sadness. After a few seconds she suddenly began to cry. [...] As the display continued she began talking about how deeply sad she felt, how she had no energies left to go on living in this manner, how hopeless and exhausted she was."

What is particularly striking about this account is the specific sequence by which the display of sadness leads to the patient's feelings of sadness and finally her thoughts of sadness.

For Damasio the importance of this rare neurological incident is due to the fact that in normal conditions of research these three events happen at such a high speed that researchers are unable to identify the sequence that links them together. In this instance the episode firmly establishes the clear sequence by which emotions lead to feelings, which in turn lead to thoughts.

The distinction between emotions and feelings is that emotions are the result of external stimuli, whereas a feeling is the internalization of an emotion, a "perception of the actual body changed by emotion".

The sequence Emotion-Feeling-Thought is well worth remembering as a corrective to the tendency many of us show in privileging reason over emotion. Often we even try to suppress our emotions by placing them in a rational stranglehold. However, this is never a good idea: it is energy-consuming and can lead to all kinds of psychic stress. Actually, as Damasio has shown, our emotions increase the efficiency of the reasoning process, making it speedier. They alert us to situations that require immediate attention. Although some of their messaging might be over-dramatic (think of jealousy, or fear of public speaking), in evolutionary terms these kinds of alerts had value. When making decisions, we may need to question some of our emotional responses and work out why we are having them, but to ignore them or try to smother them will be counterproductive.

Damasio's sequence of Emotion-Feeling-Thought is reminiscent of the 17th-century philosopher Baruch Spinoza's sequence of Will-Appetite-Desire, which underpins his concept of *conatus*. What Spinoza means by *conatus* is the drive within each of us which makes us want to realize ourselves, since "each thing strives to persevere in its being".

For Spinoza, the *conatus* is what we term *will* when associated with the mind alone. This becomes *appetite* when linked with both the mind and the body. Then, when the appetite is consciously experienced, that becomes *desire*.

Both the roads leading to Thought (in Damasio's sequence) and to Desire (in Spinoza's sequence) involve an interplay between mind and body. In what way does this similarity inform our present quest for an understanding of Momentum, and ultimately of decision making?

Well, Spinoza offers a really fascinating insight here. His definition of desire as an "appetite conscious of itself" implies the elevation to consciousness of something which we experience through our body initially, then through our mind. This leads him to a remarkable assertion: "We neither strive for, wish, seek, nor desire anything because we think it is good, but, on the contrary, we adjudge a thing to be good because we strive for, wish, seek, or desire it." Happiness comes not from receiving what we desire, but from the desires we have in the first place. Our decision making therefore becomes the exercise of the complete self, making its choices and finding a natural rightness – or goodness – following on from them.

Importantly, such a judgement has no explicit moral message. I simply realize that something is potentially good (or bad) for me. If good, it colludes with me in an arrangement that elevates me, and helps me persevere in my being, and thus experience joy.

In this way, Spinoza avoids the pitfall of opposing reason to passion. Reason has desire at its heart. This is a radical departure from the view held by Plato, illustrated by his allegory of the charioteer.

"Let us then liken the soul to the natural union of a team of winged horses and their charioteer [...]. To begin with, our driver is in charge of a pair of horses; second, one of his horses is beautiful and good and from stock of the same sort, while the other is the opposite and has the opposite sort of bloodline. This means that chariot-driving in our case is inevitably a painfully difficult business."

In Plato's allegory, the charioteer can only make progress if he keeps both horses going in the same direction: the noble, well-bred horse, which represents our rational and moral inclinations, and the more unruly horse, which symbolizes our passions and desires. This idea seems to anticipate, more than two millennia later, Freud's model of the mind, with the *ego* as the driver, the *superego* as our rational noble inclinations, and the *id* as the dark side of our personality.

What replaces the debate between reason and passion, for Spinoza, is another model based on two affects: joy versus sadness. If reason alone cannot guide us toward our best decisions, perhaps our optimal strategy is to influence our desires and adjust their trajectories in the direction of more joy (or at least less sadness). The only way to achieve this is through other, more powerful desires: "An affect cannot be restrained nor removed unless by an opposed and stronger affect".

Therefore, if we follow this path, decision making isn't the cold process of rationalizing consciously every choice we make (since we will never know all the causes behind things). Instead, Spinoza offers an approach that involves the elevation of our being through the choices we make; and the simple test of this is the joy it brings us, through the deeper connections we create within as well as around ourselves.

The Momentum "drive belt": lower half

In the previous section we established that the neuroscientist (Damasio) and the philosopher (Spinoza) agree on a major aspect of the human mind's operations: we decide first, and only then do we deliberate.

Since we often hear that decisions are a matter of *judgement*, I believe that a good analogy for decision making is the way the justice system operates in many countries. First there is a discovery process, including the deposition of witnesses; then, once the facts have been put forward, there is a deliberation by judge and jury.

Applied to decision making, the discovery process is the bringing to consciousness of emotions, feelings and desires. The resulting thoughts are then put through the process of deliberation in order to reach a final decision.

How does this compare with the model we constructed in Part II, the COSARC pyramid with its six chambers of Creation, Options, Selection, Action, Resolve and Completion? Superficially, it may seem that the *logical* COSARC model contradicts the *psychological* Emotion/Feeling/Thought model, whereby we decide first and deliberate next. However, there is in fact a valuable co-ordination between the two models.

Let us return to our judiciary analogy. If the discovery process, the formation of a decision, is made up of the elevation of emotions and feelings into a thought (or decision), then the COSARC pyramid provides the deliberation chambers where this thought is further refined. In this inner Court of Justice there is an antechamber to the COSARC pyramid, where decisions are formed before we even attempt to handle them consciously. What we now know is that by the time we consciously prepare ourselves to contemplate our options, our psyche has already decided on its choice.

At this stage, though, we have explored only one half of the Momentum "drive belt". Both the "Emotion/Feeling/Thought" sequence and its Spinozan double, the "Will/Appetite/Desire" sequence, leave us with "thought" as unrealized and "desire" as unfulfilled.

However, Spinoza did not see much point in desires remaining unsatisfied and thoughts remaining abstract, not yet applied to the real world: "No one can desire to be happy, to act well and live well, who does not at the same time desire to be, to act, and to live, that is to say, actually to exist."

As we are exploring the link between emotion and action, we are bound to ask ourselves: where is the potentially weak point in this link? Where does the line break, on those occasions when our desires do not lead to action or when our thoughts are not followed through? Moreover, how can we resolve the conflict between what we want and what we do – between our being and our life?

This question is beautifully answered by Martin Buber in *The Way of Man*. For Buber, the true origin of any conflict lies in the essential conflict between three principles in man's being and life: the principle of *thought*, the principle of *speech*, and the principle of *action*". He continues:

"The origin of all conflicts between me and my fellow-men is that I do not say what I mean, and that I do not do what I say. […] By our contradiction, our lie, we foster conflict situations and give them power over us until they enslave us. From here, there is no way out but by the crucial realization: everything depends on myself, and the crucial decision: I will straighten myself out."

Elsewhere in the same essay Buber writes of the importance of beginning with oneself. This personal focus should receive our full attention, since otherwise our initiative would be weakened and our whole undertaking frustrated.

With Buber we reach a form of "closure" regarding our Momentum chain or drive-belt. What completes the Emotion-Feeling-Thought loop is Buber's Thought-Speech-Action sequence, so that the full chain goes:

Emotion-Feeling-Thought-Speech-Action

Buber seems to echo Edgar's redemptive words at the end of Shakespeare's *King Lear*: "Speak what we feel, not what we ought to say."

This line also highlights the critical "missing link" revealed to us by Buber: *Speech*, the articulation and affirmation of our thoughts and desires. Verbalization of thought is the moment when an idea is brought by and through us from the stream of emotions and feelings into the reality of the world, to occupy the same space that we, as humans, live in and share: language. This process is the key to enacting our resolve.

ORIENTATION POINT

Verbalizing can make a crucial breakthrough in decision making, even when we are thinking and acting alone. We are, after all, engaged in a perpetual inner dialogue, often mixing words, emotions and feelings in a fuzzy mental swarm. One way of sifting the mix is to express your thinking more precisely, in language, as if you were composing a précis for yourself. Often just a single phrase, accurately expressed, can give you a useful compass bearing in your decision making.

What Buber warns us against is a virtual world where decisions remain ideas, and do not materialize – a world where we may think one thing, say another, and enact yet another one besides. If Momentum consists in the uninterrupted displacement of will through the Emotion-Feeling-Thought-Speech-Action chain, any disruption along the way will breach this Momentum. Inconsistencies between thought, speech and action are the main culprits. Also potentially disruptive is any disconnection from our emotions, feelings and desires. Buber's exhortation to begin with oneself, and "to care about nothing in the world than this beginning", serves as a reminder that the starting point of good decision making is always going to be an aligned, individuated psyche. It also means that struggles to decide can be linked to some deeper, inner tensions – a theme we explored earlier.

The Momentum chain gives dynamism to a life force. Both Spinoza and Damasio concluded that the taming into submission of our passions and desires equates to the weakening of this life force, and ultimately its interruption.

On this note, it would not have escaped Spinoza that the word for "interruption" in biblical Hebrew is the same word meaning "misfortune" or "adversity". We interrupt the Momentum chain at our peril.

Let us remember that the mythical character representing the uninterrupted passage of time, Chronos, is often represented holding a scythe, the instrument also used in the iconography of Death. And what is a scythe if not the instrument of a radical separation? This is exactly what our most difficult decisions demand.

As it turns out, if the Momentum chain carries our life force, it will necessarily be interrupted one last time, by death, the interruption of all interruptions. Maybe it is no coincidence that the French expression for "still life" is *nature morte* – "dead nature".

But there are two ways to look at death. In a biological way, death signifies the end of our body as a living organism. In a Spinozan way, death is any interruption of our desire. We die in those moments, whether fractions of seconds or days on end, when our desire is muffled, silent, absent or void.

It follows that life is not only the sum of our decisions; it is also primarily the sum of our desires.

Carl Jung observed that "the spirit of evil is negation of the life force by fear. Only boldness can deliver us from fear, and if the risk is not taken, the meaning of life is violated." We have seen earlier how damaging fear can be as a deterrent to even starting our decision making. Once we *have* made a start, fear can throw us off course. In his reference to "boldness" Jung offers the beginning of a solution. In the realm of decisions, a close synonym for this is *intentionality*, "the fact of being deliberate or purposive" (as the *Oxford Dictionary* defines it). This is the source of all flow experiences.

Intentionality matters a great deal to decision making because it is the purest and most original manifestation of our will, of our *conatus*. This is what we need in order to quieten our fears. It is the energy that moves the roadblocks of fear from our chosen path. It is what reveals our will and, at the same time, unleashes the power of Momentum.

Seizing this energy, the power of our will, is the theme of this book's next and final part.

KEY SKILL 4

HOW TO ACCEPT THE UNCHANGEABLE AND CHANGE THE UNACCEPTABLE

"It is only by relinquishing control over what is beyond our power that we can fully experience flow …" (see page 106)

A key precept in life is that we must accept what cannot be changed, and apply our efforts to change what we can for the better. In any context – business or life in general – this includes seeking self-improvement to release the qualities that make us special. More obviously, it involves changing the surrounding circumstances – for example, picking the right team for a project, setting the right goals, motivating team members, doing all you can to ensure maximum efficiency.

Processing
It is important in business not to waste energy deciding to bring about unrealistic changes. It is obvious you cannot change another country's laws. However, it is less obvious you cannot change a company's location: maybe you can, despite the costs.

Good managers avoid making instant judgements based on apparent implausibility. A situation that has lasted a long time looks increasingly unalterable – a psychological effect one might term the "time-weighted value of the given". At a deep level of the psyche, the imagination is daunted: it feels change would require pitching oneself against history, expressed in the status quo.

Clearly, such thinking is flawed: the emotional response (lapse of confidence) needs to be set aside in any feasibility study. There will, of course, be many occasions when a project does indeed turn out not to be feasible. Here, the opposite problem may occur, namely attachment to a personal vision, an unwillingness to stop trying. Again, detachment skills are needed to arrive at a good decision.

Other people are often a big factor in decision making. To know how to influence others you need empathy; then to exert the necessary influence you need to be a strong and sensitive communicator, matching your approach to the person concerned.

Sometimes, rather than making a direct approach, a better strategy is to apply the lever of influence via a third party, perhaps someone closer than you are to the individual in question.

Guidelines for acceptance

A basic law of life and business is that *acceptance prompts the need for changes.* These changes may be classified as follows:

- *Work on the self*
  Identify your emotions and choose a positive response to them. The best response is to accept those emotions in a spirit of self-forgiveness while making positive choices unemotionally. These positive choices, if embraced wholeheartedly, will not allow space for damaging energies such as regret or resentment.
- *Work on the impacts*
  Identify the effects of acceptance on you and others, and plan what you need to do to minimize the downsides and maximize the upsides. Carry out those plans in a positive spirit.
- *Work on the future*
  Do not let the situation you have accepted be defining: acceptance is not where you live. You have an open future still, in which to make new plans and find the best possible expression for your core strengths. Let the future be a blossoming of the Self.

Guidelines for change

Change is life-giving oxygen for the brave. Work on your personal qualities by stretching and thereby strengthening them. In particular, you will need self-esteem, imagination, resourcefulness, resilience, empathy, courage and good communication skills. Plan any major change as a set of small sub-changes. Understand the bigger picture (step back to see it whole) but do not be daunted by it: any big picture is made up of smaller parts, so in concentrating on one part you are honouring the situation's reality.

PART IV

THE DECIDING MIND

CHAPTER 10
A QUESTION OF PERSPECTIVE

The period from the 14th to the 17th century in Europe, which we know as the Renaissance, was an era not so much of new discoveries as of *re*-discoveries – of ideas from Greek and Roman antiquity.

In particular, there was a new humanism at work, prompted by the rediscovery of classical philosophers. Among these was Protagoras, who in the 5th century BC had famously expressed the view that "man is the measure of all things".

The inspiration of antiquity was felt not only in philosophy but also in such diverse fields as painting, architecture, literature and science. In art, for example, the idea of linear perspective gained currency. A connection with decision making soon suggests itself. Perspective depends on a viewpoint from which distant things appear smaller. And we all know that our most challenging decisions require us to adopt a new perspective in order to escape the deadlock of indecision. Therefore, the topic of perspective merits closer attention.

There is plenty of evidence showing that the ability to render a lifelike view of nature in painting and sculpture had already been mastered by great artists of the antiquity. Already in the 5th century BC a Greek scene painter, Agatharchus, wrote a commentary on his use of convergent perspective, which had a broad following among his contemporaries.

After centuries of approximate and somewhat naive representation of perspective in medieval art, Renaissance artists had available plenty of historic precedents to inspire their representation of nature.

Filippo Brunelleschi (1377–1446) was an Italian architect widely credited with rediscovering linear perspective. This technique allowed him to come up with such creative designs as the famous dome of Florence Cathedral, still a feat of engineering by today's standards.

Shortly after Brunelleschi's rediscovery of linear perspective, it became the standard practice in studios throughout Western Europe. This trend was accelerated by the publication in 1435 of Leon Battista Alberti's treatise *On Painting*. Here Alberti formalizes Brunelleschi's successful experiences with linear perspective into a fully fledged theory.

Alongside these artistic developments, the Renaissance created a parallel revolution in philosophy. For the best part of a thousand years, since the 12th century, philosophical thinking in Western Europe had been the domain of the Catholic Church. Then came the rediscovery of the ancient Greek schools of philosophy, such as Platonism, Aristotelianism, Stoicism, Epicureanism and Scepticism (a philosophy that recommends doubting the existence of God). Not surprisingly, these ideas were seen as direct threats by the Church, who responded with the accusation of heresy, leading, in many cases to excommunication, even execution.

However, while the Church was seen as actively resisting such new ideas, it was far from immune to their influence. Under the patronage of Julius II, Michelangelo painted the ceiling of the Sistine Chapel, and Raphael was commissioned to decorate the Vatican Stanze. These are among the masterworks that best symbolize the High Renaissance in Rome.

These incredible paintings all have one thing in common: a superior command of perspective. This is highly visible in, for example, *The School of Athens*, Raphael's masterpiece. In this large fresco, Raphael uses the technique of the one-point perspective to magnify the sense of architectural grandeur while at the same time giving a heightened aura to the Greek philosophers depicted, and by implication to their intellectual achievements.

In turn, the patronage by the Church of leading Renaissance artists could not have happened without some of the Renaissance's not only artistic, but also philosophical ideas, infiltrating its tightly preserved dogma.

We can observe, for example, that the way in which the arts embraced linear perspective and, in turn, the Church embraced the arts, led to some of its theologians being inspired, consciously or not, by the notion of perspective in their own writings.

One notable example is St Ignatius, born as Íñigo López de Loyola, the founder of the Society of Jesus, the Jesuit order. Born in 1491, one year before Columbus's discovery of America, when Europe was transitioning from the Early to the High Renaissance, he was influential at a time when the Catholic faith was challenged by the Reformation and the likes of Luther and Calvin. Resisting such tendencies, Ignatius became one of the figureheads of the Counter-Reformation. He understood the need to return to the scriptures in their purest form, and to establish a more direct link with God.

Underlying his concept of "discernment of spirits" is the idea that God communicates directly with each of us through our feelings, desires and thoughts. Distinguishing those feelings that emanate from God from those that do not is critical to Ignatius's teachings. Where do our feelings, thoughts and desires emanate from? And how can knowing this help us make the right decisions? These are some of the questions that Ignatius aims to answer in his *Spiritual Exercises*.

ORIENTATION POINT

If we understand where our feelings, desires, thoughts and fears come from, we are better placed to make decisions that serve us effectively. This idea was explored by Ignatius of Loyola in his *Spiritual Exercises*. A questioning form of self-analysis is always a good starting-point for decision making, since it respects one of the key principles of human behaviour: the idea that our choices are presented to us not in a vacuum but as natural extensions of a fully lived life.

Overall, Ignatius's approach invites us to look at decisions "from every point of view", and to be patient with the process. In addition, he recommends that for every decision, we should draw up a list of positive versus negative considerations for each option. Should this fail to deliver a clear decision, he then suggests that we consult with other people whom we trust, and also that we learn to trust our own hearts. Ultimately, when no clear answer emerges, decision making is about looking "to which side reason most inclines, and thus [...] according to the stronger movement of the reason", taking a leap of faith.

Three techniques

There are three specific techniques in *Spiritual Exercises* that caught my attention. In the first of these, Ignatius suggests that we distance ourselves from our preferred choice to consider our options objectively and "should be as though at the centre of a pair of scales". To help us maintain focus and perspective, he asks us "to keep as [our] objective the end for which [we were] created".

In another passage, Ignatius suggests that we imagine "a person whom [we] have never seen or known [...] for whom [we] desire full perfection", and who needs to make the same decision as we do. He recommends that we then picture ourselves providing advice to this person on their decision. The underlying idea is that we are better at advising others than we are at following our own advice. What is implied is that this added distance and perspective can help us with our own thinking: "Then as my case is the same, I should do the same myself, and keep the rule that I lay down for another."

ORIENTATION POINT

If you imagine you are advising a stranger on the best course of action in a situation that mirrors your own, the "distance" involved in this can help you make a good decision for yourself. This is an excellent approach to take when the effort of self-analysis seems more than you can manage at the moment – for example, because your issues are particularly complex or painful.

The third of these suggestions – and the most powerful in my mind, albeit more sinister too – is to imagine ourselves "at the point of death", on our last day, about to face divine judgement. "I should look at and consider my situation on the Day of Judgment, and think how at that moment I would want to have chosen in the present matter; and adopt now the rule that I would then want to have observed [...]." With this in mind – the ultimate hindsight – which course of action would we be most proud of?

In each of these suggestions, the common link is distance and perspective: distancing ourselves from our preferences, from our egos, and from our living selves; and gaining clarity and insight from that remote position.

Ignatius demonstrated extraordinary prescience in his emphasis on the value of distancing ourselves: most authors writing on decision making today, 500 years later, echo his view that we can gain clarity and insight by taking an artificially remote position.

Distance is a technique suggested by most self-help manuals, including Chip and Dan Heath's *Decisive: How to make better decisions*. The Heath brothers, who teach at Stanford Graduate School of Business and Duke University, recommend using their "WRAP" formula when facing challenging decisions. It involves these four steps:

- **W**iden your options.
- **R**eality-test your assumptions.
- **A**ttain distance before deciding.
- **P**repare to be wrong.

The reference in the third step to the importance of distance chimes with the point implied by St Ignatius. But how do these authors suggest we attain that distance?

First, we need to beware of the influence of our immediate emotions – something Ignatius would have wholeheartedly agreed with. One way of achieving this distance from our present emotions is the 10-10-10 method, which forces us to pay attention to future emotions as much as present ones. This tool was invented by Suzy Welch, the American author and business journalist. It goes through the three time frames we may benefit from considering when facing a decision. These are; How will I feel about this 10 minutes from making this decision? How will I feel after 10 months? And, finally, after 10 years?

Such reflections would not be a negation of emotions. Rather, this technique is meant to distance us from our *short-term* emotions, placing them in the perspective afforded by our medium-term and long-term ones.

Self-knowledge, of course, must be available for us to be able to make the necessary projections into the future. However, even with this element of self-awareness, the method – like any perspective – relies on an illusion: in reality, we cannot claim real awareness of our emotions today, let alone in 10 months' or 10 years' time. Still, the method at least steps back and provides a degree of distance, for all its imperfections.

Later in their book the Heath brothers suggest: "Perhaps the most powerful question for resolving personal decisions is: What would I tell my best friend to do in this situation?" I wonder if they realized, when writing these words, they were revisiting Ignatius's injunction of 1524! Ignatius, however, went further, suggesting that we imagine advising a stranger rather than a friend, in order to create an even greater distance.

There is another aspect of the Heaths' book that recalls Ignatius's *Spiritual Exercises*. Sensibly, these authors explain that agonizing decisions often spring from a conflict among our priorities, and that if we wish "to pursue our core priorities, we must go on the offence against lesser priorities".

We find a similar idea in *Spiritual Exercises*, where in the matter of decision making Ignatius tells us there are three types of people, each with a distinctive attitude:

- *All talk and no action*
  This kind of person is well-intentioned but easily distracted by a whole range of relatively inconsequential issues. Not to decide ends up being their decision.

- *Doing everything except …*
  This type of person does everything except what is necessary. Though active, these people enact only those decisions that do not ask too much of them, not the decisions that are aligned with their true calling.
- *Whole-hearted*
  This type of person is the one Ignatius describes as truly free. "Their whole and deepest desire is to do whatever God's will is for them with no conditions attached."

More recently, Professor Joseph Badaracco of Harvard Business School has written an article entitled "How to tackle your toughest decisions". Here he explains that there are five questions we should ask ourselves in order to improve our judgement:

- *What are the net, net consequences of all my options?*
  This is about asking ourselves, if necessary with the help of trusted advisors and experts, what every option would lead to, and keeping an open mind about why each option could potentially be the best.
- *What are my core obligations?*
  Here we are asked to consider our main duties, to family, friends, employees and so on. You need to work out specifically what these duties require you to do in any particular situation. Badaracco recommends you step aside from your comfort zone, identify your biases and blind spots and empathically project yourself into the position of all key stakeholders, especially those who are most vulnerable.
- *What will work in the world as it is?*
  As Badaracco reminds us, the concept of "the world as it is" points toward Niccolò Machiavelli's *The Prince* – a key work of the Florentine Renaissance. This book had the explicit purpose of showing rulers how to survive in the world *as it is* and not *as it should be*. Applied to decision making, this concept involves testing our ideas against the reality of the world, with all its unyielding facts and gritty surfaces, where perfect theories do not always translate into perfect practice.
- *Who are we?*
  This is a question about our values. As an individual, as an institution, as a corporation, or as any other group of people, what do we stand for? And in what way is any option that is available faithful or otherwise to those values?

- *What can we live with?*
  The final question is about the acceptability of the option we finally chose. How comfortable do we feel about living with that choice in the future? (We are reminded here of Suzy Welch's 10-10-10 method, described on page 127.)

The reference to Machiavelli is not the only reminiscence of the Renaissance. I find it striking that some of Badaracco's questions echo, almost literally, what Ignatius wrote five centuries earlier.

For example, when in response to his first question Badaracco recommends thinking about net consequences, he adds: "So your job is to put aside your initial assumption about what you *should* do, [....] and ask yourself: What *could* we do?" In other words, objectively consider *all* the options available. Is this not similar to Ignatius's suggestion that we distance ourselves from our preferred option, and "try to be like a balance at equilibrium, without leaning to either side"?

Also, when considering the answer to the fourth question, *Who are we?*, Badaracco suggests we imagine ourselves writing a sentence or a chapter in our own history. This is highly reminiscent of Ignatius's idea of imagining yourself on your last day.

And when it comes to the fifth question, *What can I live with?*, Badaracco's advice is to "imagine yourself explaining your decision to a close friend or mentor". Here again, we are reminded of Ignatius's suggestion that we imagine ourselves giving advice to another person faced with the same dilemma. Ignatius goes even further, in making the other a projection of ourselves – an *alter ego* – rather than a mere counterpart or a sounding board.

What we find in a whole range of approaches, again and again, from Ignatius's *Spiritual Exercises* to the present day's self-help manuals, are these notions of distance and perspective.

However, perspective is – and has always been – the *illusion* that what we see is what is out there. In short, it gives the illusion of objectivity. In decision making, however, perspective can be more than an illusion: it can serve a greater purpose, helping us make better decisions in the real world.

To understand this point, we need to return to Brunelleschi. The artist's original intention behind his rediscovery of linear perspective was to use a two-dimensional representation of reality in order to create a three-dimensional monument – a building – in the real world. The illusion, in this case, served to design, build and perfect something real.

Leon Battista Alberti, aged 32, wrote his treatise *On Painting* in 1435, dedicating it to Brunelleschi, who was 59. This is the first modern treatise on the theory of painting, and in it Alberti formalizes the newly rediscovered technique of perspective.

First, we must note that Alberti's yardstick is always nature, as the perfect representation of a divinely inspired order. The purpose of painting or architecture is to offer the most perfect representation of natural beauty, which he defines in another treaty, more than 20 years later: "Beauty is a form of sympathy and consonance of the parts within a body, according to definite number, outline and position, as dictated by *concinnitas*, the absolute and fundamental rule of Nature." The level of perfection and harmony that is *concinnitas* happens when "nothing may be added, taken away or altered, but for the worse". (This is highly reminiscent of Gerhard Richter's reflection about his art, more than 500 years later: see page 92.)

At the same time, Alberti was influenced by Protagoras's view that "man is the mean and the measure of all things". Therefore, if perfection exists in nature, it is essentially subjective, in that it is a function of how a person apprehends it, and in turn represents it. For Alberti, man is "the mean or measure" of perspectival representation.

What does this mean in practice? Alberti writes:

> "Let me tell you what I do when I am painting. First of all, on the surface on which I am going to paint, I draw a rectangle of whatever size I want, which I regard as an open window through which the subject to be painted is seen. And I decide how large I wish the human figure in the painting to be."

Now, perspective in painting can be taken as a metaphor for perspective in decision making. So let us look at the implications of Alberti's method for our understanding of the deciding mind.

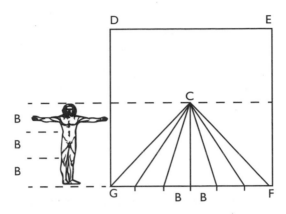

Alberti's method in drawing perspective was to start with the picture area, put in a human figure as a starting point, then use this figure's dimensions as the basis for converging lines within which the picture would be composed.

The view through a window

The first step, according to Alberti, is the delineation of a rectangle which he refers to as an "open window", through which the subject is seen.

If perspective matters in decision making, then the first step needs to be the framing of a future decision – what is the horizon we are contemplating, within which a decision will happen? What are the limiting factors set by us, by other people or by the realities of the situation?

The notion of framing is so important in the arts that to this day the vast majority of paintings are rectangular, which make it possible to frame them easily. The "frame" that is the canvas is itself hung in a wooden frame, and some frames are works of art in their own right. It is as if we needed to be reminded that the decision regarding the space to be delineated is as important as the choice of subject. Also, a frame is – to use Alberti's expression – a "window": it serves the purpose of separating the outside world from whatever happens inside the painting. The frame is an invitation to step into another world, surreptitiously – not through the main door but through a ground-floor window, at our height, which puts us in a unique position to get involved. In a way, every painting is a *trompe-l'œil*.

ORIENTATION POINT

Perspective lines to a vanishing point within the "window" of a frame give a useful analogy for effective decision making. A 360-degree view is not helpful. We need to focus on what is relevant. Some decision-makers swamp their own vision of a situation by trying to master a too detailed and comprehensive picture of the context. Better to be selective, following one's intuitive judgement.

Through the illusion of perspective, it feels as if, from the moment we step into the painting through the window created by the frame, we will see that scene in its entirety.

As we saw earlier, when making decisions, we often feel we need more information – ideally a 360-degree vision of the situation. What this analogy implies, however, is that the opposite is true: unless we frame a decision, which means focusing on the *main* scene, excluding peripheral information, we will lack a focal point. This is because the vanishing point described by Alberti needs the outer lines of the frame in order to exist. Without the limits they set, there can be no central point, and no focus either.

Making decisions does not require us knowing, or caring about, everything about a given situation: instead, we must know and care *just enough*. In Alberti's model, the painter – and by analogy for us the decision-maker – starts the entire process with this initial consideration: what is the scope of my decision?

There are many examples where a decision is made difficult, sometimes even impossible, by the inclusion of too many stakeholders and conflicting viewpoints. Owning our decisions implies framing the scope of what we should concern ourselves with, versus what we shouldn't.

The scope of a decision will also include the time we give ourselves to execute it. Sometimes, the timing is imposed on us: there is a deadline to observe. But when this is not the case, when the horizon line is blurred, we should set ourselves a time-frame within which to make our decision. Without such delineation we are giving ourselves an open-ended invitation to procrastinate, whilst we are busy blaming our own busyness. As if we were an artist, our first concern should be the selection of a canvas of the right dimension.

Chasing the vanishing point

I was surprised, when reading Alberti's treatise, to discover that its first chapter opens with a definition of the word "point". Precisely because this feels unnecessary and self-evident, it probably is the opposite – and highly symbolic too.

> "The first thing to know is that a point is a sign which one might say is not divisible into parts. I call a sign anything which exists on a surface so that it is visible to the eye. The only exception to this last condition is the vanishing point, which precisely because of its disappearing nature may be implied rather than physically visible on the canvas, but one could argue that it is made all the more present through its strongly implied absence."

Returning to our analogy with decisions, the vanishing point is an apt symbol for something else which is by nature indivisible and can only be defined by its absence: the Self. Like the vanishing point, the Self is invisible, indivisible and undefinable. For Jung it is and will always remain a mystery. At best, it can be approximated as the centre of the total personality, which includes consciousness, the unconscious and the ego. Let us remember the etymology of the word "individual": "that which cannot be divided".

This idea of using the vanishing point as a symbol for the Self is probably easier to accept when thinking of a portrait, where it seems to point toward the sitter's psyche. However, the parallel also applies to landscape or even abstract paintings. The vanishing point is where all the elements converge – often in a manner that is symbolic of the artist's psychological state.

Centre of clarity

Alberti's ideas about the so-called "centric ray" also give decision-makers food for thought. The centric ray had been defined by Ptolemy, in the context of geometrical optics, as the ray that does not get refracted.

Here is what Alberti has to say about it:

> "It is of all the rays undoubtedly the most keen and vigorous. It is also true that a quantity will never appear larger than when the centric ray rests upon it. A great deal could be said about the power and function of this ray. One thing should not go unsaid: the ray alone is supported in their midst, like a united assembly, by all the others, so that it must rightly be called the leader and prince of rays."

The question posed by this optical concept, when applied to decision making, is: which aspects of our decisions feature on the centric way? Are we giving prominence to those considerations that are critical, or are we allowing secondary concerns to feature there, blurring our vision?

Too often, the centric ray is blurred by such considerations as other people's agendas in relation to our own; minor consequences of our actions versus the main benefits; fear versus courage; and so on. Alberti then goes on to discuss *arrangement* – which objects should be positioned where. So it goes with decisions. It befalls on us to compose – or arrange – our thoughts with as much care and focus. Some considerations will need to be excluded from our field of view; but among those thoughts that remain "in scope", we should have a clear vision of priorities.

ORIENTATION POINT

The phrase "centric ray" is a useful reminder of the importance of undistorted vision. The precise scientific definition is unimportant: if you imagine how light is distorted unless it comes directly into the viewer's eye along a central line of sight you will get the general idea. Looking along the centric ray requires you to have the wisdom and courage to face the reality of the prospects in front of you – without any bias from yourself or others.

Adding light and colour

Anybody who has ever stood in front of a painting by Caravaggio or any other master of chiaroscuro will have witnessed at first hand the power of light and shadow in the dramatic tension represented by the painter.

Chiaroscuro, which literally means "lightdark" in Italian (without a space or a hyphen in between), seems to signify even graphically, through the contraction of two words into one, that light and darkness are one and the same thing.

This thought, recalling Heraclitus in his assertion that day and night are one, has a physical reality in the arts: the angle and intensity with which light falls upon an object forms a shadow of corresponding shape and depth.

Alberti captures this thought when exploring the different uses of light and shadow and how they reveal different facets of an object or a subject.

Similarly, in our decision making, the choice of lighting influences what we see and what we miss. We may therefore want to observe the scene "in a different light" before committing to a decision. Some types of lighting are more illuminating than others, showing the most harmonious and meaningful picture of the matter in hand.

Light is also what, in the eye of someone looking at a painting, transforms a two-dimensional surface into the illusion of a three-dimensional object. Light creates depth. When we cast new light on our choices, we reach a new depth in our ability to decide.

Lighting that is different in intensity, direction or distance creates a different shadow. This is highly reminiscent of the use of the shadow image in psychology, principally by Carl Jung. In Jungian psychology the Shadow is the "dark side", the unconscious aspect of the personality that the ego does not accept or identify.

"Everyone carries a shadow," Jung wrote, "and the less it is embodied in the individual's conscious life, the blacker and denser it is." In other words, refusing to see the truth about oneself is inherently destructive – of our decisions as well as our general well-being.

All the greatest works of art, whether paintings, photographs or even sculptures, create a uniquely masterful combination of light and shadow. Often, the most significant quality is not the intensity of the light they use but its subtlety, resulting from the softening and contrasting contribution of shadow. The same applies to our best decisions, and certainly to our toughest decisions. Can we engage, not only with the light of our consciousness, but also with the shadowy side of our personalities? Could a present difficulty mirror a specific aspect of our Shadow? Could the facets of our personality that we do not accept be distorting our most important decisions?

Concerning the use of colour, in contrast to Aristotle who thought that all colours derive from white and black (again, light and shadow), Alberti writes:

"I would not wish to be contradicted by those more expert than myself who, while following the philosophers, nonetheless assert that in the nature of things there are only two true colours, white and black, and all the rest arise from the mixture of these two. My own view about colours, as a painter, is that from the mixture of colours there arises an almost infinite variety of others, but that for painters there are four true genera of colours corresponding to the number of the elements, and from these many species are produced. There is fire-colour, which they call red, and the colour of air which is said to be blue-grey, and the green of water, and the earth is ash-coloured."

In Alberti's view, these four primary colours, corresponding to the four elements, once combined with black and white, will recreate the infinite range of colours in nature.

This theme of colour evokes two parallels between painting and decision making.

The first concerns our intuition. Unlikely as it sounds, when facing a challenging decision, we might consider closing our eyes for a moment and asking ourselves what colour is associated with this decision, or with the various options involved. This purely intuitive shortcut into the unconscious can sometimes reveal how we truly feel about a possible choice that is available. For example, if the colour that a decision evokes is a threatening dark grey, we may choose to explore what it would take to bring in some brighter, more vivid colours onto the canvas. This kind of procedure, although not for everyone, in my experience can be surprisingly effective.

The second parallel between paintings and decisions, again on this theme of colour, is related to emotions. What are the emotions involved when you contemplate a pending decision?

In his *Ethics*, Spinoza defines 48 different types of affect, including love and hatred, hope and fear, envy and compassion. These are nearly all manifestations of the three basic affects, namely:

- *Desire* (*cupiditas*) or appetite (*appetitus*), defined as "the very essence of man".
- *Joy* (*laetitia*), defined as "man's transition from a state of less perfection to a state of greater perfection".
- *Sadness* (*tristitia*), defined as "man's transition from a state of greater perfection to a state of less perfection".

In Spinoza's view, any affect that increases a person's power of activity leads to greater perfection. In the case of decisions, the objective is exactly the same: increasing our power of activity in order to reach a higher rung, leading to greater perfection. And the emotion through which our soul achieves greater perfection is joy.

Even if Spinoza can identify 48 emotional "colours", ultimately these affects result from the combination of merely three primary affects, each time combined with more or less light or darkness, to create the full polychromatic range.

Similarly, we should question our impending decisions, testing them against our truest desires and the sense of joy or sadness they may evoke, as well as the many other affects that derive from them. This emotional test is very different from the rational way in which most people assess their decisions.

On distance

Decision making requires us to use perspective, and we have by now established, following Alberti's advice, that notions like *framing, vanishing point, light* and *colour* are all central to our understanding of this concept. However, the main aspect of perspective is bound to be the treatment of distance and proportion.

This is the greatest difference between the works of Early Renaissance artists, such as Cimabue, Uccello and Giotto, and their High Renaissance successors, from Leonardo to Raphael and beyond.

In Early Renaissance art, the treatment of perspective was tentative and approximate. This created elongated figures that seem to be detached from their backgrounds in an almost supernatural way.

By contrast, High Renaissance paintings adopt a much more precise sense of perspective. They appear considerably more realistic, whilst retaining a strong sense of the divine and the mystical. Leonardo is at the junction between these two great chapters of art history.

Two paintings, both in the Uffizi Gallery in Florence, are highly significant in this context. The first is Andrea Verrochio's *The Baptism of Christ,* c1470–75. The second is Leonardo's *Annunciation,* c1472–5. Verrochio was a highly successful artist by the time he started working on the *Baptism*. Although most of the painting was executed by him, Giorgio Vasari in his 16th-century *Lives of the Painters* claims that one of Verrochio's workshop assistants, the teenaged Leonardo da Vinci, was asked by his Master to paint the figure of the angel at the left of the picture. According to Vasari, Leonardo's contribution was so much better than the figures by his Master that Verrochio refused to ever paint again, because a child artist had far surpassed him.

Although critics consider this story to be apocryphal, it is true that the angel at the left of the painting is of a different quality, seeming to display a relief and realism that are missing from the other characters.

In the second painting, the *Annunciation*, reputed to be Leonardo's earliest major work, art historians have noted some surprising errors regarding the use of perspective. There is clearly something wrong with the position and shape of the Virgin's bookrest. Also, her right arm seems to be almost dislocated. This led certain critics to doubt the attribution to Leonardo. However, another more recent theory suggests that far from being an error of perspective, the artist instead used this technique to demonstrate a superior understanding and practice of perspective. Exponents of this idea claim that, seen from a different viewpoint (that is, not directly facing the painting), these "errors" start making sense, and are coherent with the overall scene.

This is similar to the *anamorphosis* technique used by other Renaissance artists, the most famous example being Hans Holbein's *The Ambassadors*, where at the bottom of the painting an elongated and apparently abstract shape reveals itself to be a skull – a reminder of life's finitude – the moment the viewer moves to observe the painting from the side.

However, the main difference between Leonardo's *Annunciation* and Holbein's masterpiece is that in *The Ambassadors* the use of *anamorphosis* is undoubtedly intentional, since the act of stepping sideways creates a true revelation.

With Leonardo's *Annunciation*, the distortion is less obviously deliberate, but I cannot help noticing that a slight displacement of the viewer tends to reconcile the sense of perspective among all the elements of the picture. This happens when you view the painting from the right-hand side, creating the illusion that the Virgin is static and meditative, sitting in front of the viewer, whereas the angel seems to have just flown in from heaven.

This art historical diversion may seem to have taken us a long way from decision making, but it does prompt us to observe that there is sometimes a thin line between enlightened amateurism and true genius.

Applied to our subject, it also means that we should not be too hasty when judging a decision that may seem atypical. Such outliers may be the source of our most ingenious insights.

ORIENTATION POINT

Sometimes the skilled decision-maker has good reason for what may seem superficially like an error of judgement. This can be the case when a high level of risk is taken, or when the decision appears to sacrifice the individual's most obvious interests. An example might be not completing a task to the best of one's ability in order to allow someone else to step in and take the credit. When altruism operates in decision making, it can result in surprising choices.

The previous two stories about the *Baptism* and the *Annunciation* illustrate that in around 1470–75, perspective fully becomes part of artistic language. From this point onward there exists a clear link between distance, perspective and realism in Western art.

Alberti writes with typical commonsense in his *Treatise*:

> "It does happen with some surfaces that the nearer the eye of the observer is to it, the less it sees, and the further away it is, the greater the part of the surface it sees."

Distancing ourselves from a situation will give us a greater and more comprehensive appreciation, as the eye apprehends a broader view. The trade-off is that, to use photographic idiom, we lose "definition" when the object is further from us.

Perspective gives us the illusion of distance while preserving our proximity to the object. In Alberti's words: "if a painter follows this model, the illusion will take hold that the viewing distance is much longer than it is in reality".

My suggested analogy with decision making raises this question: what does distance mean in the context of a decision?

It is easy enough to speak of the distance between ourselves and our decisions, but it is helpful to be more precise. Now, since we have established that the vanishing point of a painting may serve as a representation of the Self, a more precise question arises: are we interested in the distance between the Self and our decisions or between the ego and our decisions? Or could it be both?

Let us now create a canvas and place upon its surface a triangle composed of ego, Self and decisions. (See the graphic on page 140.)

The vertical axis ranges from *singularity* (at the bottom) to *universality* (at the top). This is because the process of making a decision always starts from the singularity of an object. We then direct our thoughts toward that object. In doing so we also elevate the object from its singularity to the universality of all similar objects. This happens until we bring it back to its singularity, where the decision will be acted upon.

What about the horizontal axis? This features *content* on the left and *action* on the right.

Content is the ideal, noumenal (a Kantian term relating to the thing as it is in itself, rather than as a phenomenon knowable by the senses) and conceptual aspect of intentionality; whereas action is its materialization in the phenomenal world. Action is the domain of the real.

The decision-making model

Decisions feature at the right-hand side of the graphic, because this is the area where they lead to action.

The ego features at the far left, because before we decide, the ego is engaged in a conceptual debate with the Self. There is an inner tension, involving the opposition or conciliation between ego and Self: do I want to do something because it will make me look good or because it is what my true inner aspirations lead me to?

The Self is in the middle – in the place reserved for the vanishing point in the theory of perspective.

Ego and decision are not only positioned in different halves of the canvas, but I would argue too that the distance between them is a constant. The only distances that vary are the distance between Self and ego, and the related distance between Self and decision.

Why, you might ask, is the distance between ego and decision a constant? We will find the answer in an analogy from another art form: drama.

Let us revisit our favourite procrastinator, Shakespeare's Hamlet.

Millions of people around the world will claim to have seen Hamlet on stage. In fact, however, no one has – not even Shakespeare himself.

You may have been lucky enough to see Ben Whishaw, David Tennant or Paapa Essiedu performing Hamlet on stage, but you have never seen Hamlet. This nuance, which is not just semantic, will assist us greatly with the present question.

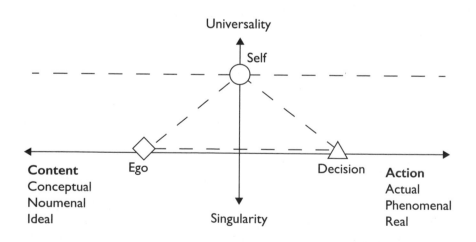

The distance between the actor who performs the role of Hamlet and Hamlet's decisions remains the same, irrespective of which actor is on stage. Hamlet's lines are written in the play's script and (ignoring a few variations in Shakespeare's different versions of the play), the lines – and the decisions they reflect – are unalterable. A play in which Hamlet would be the decisive avenger of his father, liquidating the new King in the immediate aftermath of his father's death, could not be called *Hamlet*.

This is why the distance between actor and decision is constant. In my analogy, the actor represents our ego, the part of us that wears a different mask to engage different audiences.

The ego never really fights a decision: it is involved in a debate with the Self. Similarly, it never tries to hide from a decision: it hides from the Self.

The struggle to decide is always a struggle with the Self; ideally it is also a struggle *for* the Self.

If the actor has no bearing on the decision (or on actions in general, which are all the fruit of decisions), what is it that makes some actors more effective than others?

Denis Diderot offered an answer to this question in the 18th century. In *Le Paradoxe du Comédien*, the philosopher expresses the view that the less the actor feels when on stage, the more he can make the audience feel. Diderot wants to see a significant distance between the actor and the essence of the role (in our analogy, between ego and Self).

At the other end of this spectrum, we find a different school of thought in contemporary "method acting". Contrary to Diderot's view, this approach requires that actors fully identify with the role.

However, even in method acting, the distance of actor-decision or of actor-script remains a constant. One may wonder if the method actor creates a more credible, meaningful or revelatory rendition of the role. I believe that the difference between actors' talents (that is, their ability to make the role more credible and meaningful) is not a function of which method they use. If the method does make a difference, it is in terms of whence the actor is performing the role: from the character's Self (in method acting) or from the ego (in Diderot's theory).

Because Hamlet, like any human being, has both facets to his psyche, both ways of performing the role can be equally credible and meaningful. They do, however, bring a completely different light onto the role.

Having described the Ego-Self-Decision model, let us now further explore its implications for our understanding of decision making.

We have established that the distance between ego and decision is a constant. What this implies is that any time we spend trying to get closer to a decision, or to the heart of a decision, is time wasted if this is driven by the ego. We will never narrow this gap. The best we can do is to move the decision in the direction of the right of the chart, as far away as possible from conceptual/ideal (that is, the "what could be") and toward reality (the "what is"). The ego can play its role in this process, by making progress (horizontally) toward the Self. It does this either in a "self-effacing" way, whereby the ego disappears in favour of the Self; or by aligning itself with the Self, and thereby bringing the decision to its optimal place for realization. This also implies that by focusing on the decision itself and its materialization, rather than on "what's in it for the ego", we will derive the same kind of positive outcome.

In both cases, this is all about dropping the ego's guard.

On this theme, let us return to the story of Ulysses in the *Odyssey*. On his long journey home from Troy, he confronts the giant Polyphemus, who has been actively engaged in killing Ulysses's men in order to eat them, while keeping the best of them – Ulysses – for last. When the giant asks our hero for his name, Ulysses has the presence of mind to answer: "Nobody".

Later, while Polyphemus is asleep, Ulysses blinds him with a burning wooden stake. Polyphemus shouts for help, and the other giants rush to his rescue. Horrified by the scene and seeking revenge, they ask Polyphemus who was responsible for blinding him, to which he answers: "Nobody". Hence, Ulysses saves his own life.

Incidentally, when Ulysses finally reaches Ithaca, his home, at the end of his long adventure, he is recognized only by his dog, Argos. There seems to be nothing left of the outer layer of his former self, while at the same time his inner self has reached mythical hero status.

Both stories show that even for Ulysses, the hero of Homer's Odyssey, personal success (in this case, survival) involves episodes of ego denial. The same is true of our decisions.

Think of the example of a student who has the choice between two universities, each offering a different subject: Law and Astrophysics. Let us assume this student is equally interested in both subjects and cannot decide between them.

If her decision is motivated by ego considerations, she may be preoccupied by the following questions:

- Which will give me a better career and status?
- Which will make me or my family prouder?

> ## ORIENTATION POINT
>
> Distancing yourself from your decisions, and judging whether they are right for you, is no easy task. You need to understand the difference between the requirements of the ego and those of the Self. In simplified terms, the ego's perspective is narrow, close-focusing, short-term, whereas the Self's view is broad, far-seeing, long-term. That does not mean that the ego is intrinsically wrong: sometimes, in the practicalities of a decision, you need to be focused and to ignore the bigger picture. However, the Self embraces the whole context of the decision, looking at what will best serve your life, your personal journey. By dropping the ego's guard and aligning it with the Self you can judge your decisions more wisely. Expose the ego to the Self's wisdom and the Self to the ego's capability: ease the tension between the two.

My hunch is that these questions will be of no real assistance with the decision at hand.

If her choice, however, is motivated by the Self rather than the ego, she may ask herself:

- How will I feel the day after making this decision if I choose (a) Law; (b) Astrophysics?
- If I project myself into the future, depending on the direction I take, which of these two characters seems to enjoy their career more and is more fulfilled professionally?
- Which of these two options appeals more to my inner aspirations?
- If I imagine myself in 60 years, long after retirement, which decision is likely to give me the most joy?

This kind of reflection, focused on the Self, is more likely to break the deadlock of procrastination.

Alternatively, we can achieve the same outcome by focusing on the decision rather than the implications for ego or Self. This shifting of the decision toward the right of our chart will pull the ego toward the middle, making it more aligned with the Self. This approach involves thinking about the decision in the most practical way, including, for example, each of the various steps involved in its realization.

In their book *Willpower* Roy Baumeister and John Tierney describe an experiment that tested the relative impact of *proximal* goals (that is, short-term objectives) versus *distal* goals (long-term objectives). "It turned out," they write, "that the distal goals were no better than having no goals at all. Only the proximal goals produced improvements in learning, self-efficacy and performance."

Breaking up a decision into its proximal goals is equivalent to shifting the decision toward the right of our chart. It makes it more actionable.

In Alberti's model of perspective the observer's viewpoint is critical. One question this raises, when drawing the analogy with decisions, is this: from whose viewpoint are we considering a decision?

As we have seen, we may delude ourselves when thinking that we make our own decisions, whereas we may be channelling other people's viewpoints and interests. If this is the case, we may be exercising free will, but it will be *theirs,* not *ours.*

It is our responsibility to be sole viewer and adopt a truly central position when making decisions. Granted, we should not ignore other people's views, but their role is to inform our decisions, not to hijack them. The starting point and the end point must remain with us.

This is not only about how we decide, it is also about how we *will*, and how we think. Adopting a central position equates to inhabiting our psyche. The analogy here is of the psyche as a house – an image that features regularly in our dreams. We often hear the expression "to make a house a home". Can we make our psyche a home too? Can we make it a place where we are grounded and where our decisions are aligned with our truest needs?

The French philosopher Gaston Bachelard wrote: "All really inhabited space bears the essence of the notion of a home." It is in our power to "really inhabit" that space, rather than simply dwell in it. Tough decisions can be extremely helpful if they reveal a fault line, a crack in the walls of this house: they then serve as an indication that we need to realign. They also show us what we need to attend to. The house that is a home is properly insulated and weatherproof; it is also compartmentalized without being fragmented. It is a space where the substance of decisions is well delineated, and does not risk leaking through the floors, walls or partitions.

Ultimately, decisions are the test of whether *where we are* is also *where we should be*. Do we feel we fully inhabit the house that is a home, or do we need to carry out some necessary repairs and maintenance work?

One issue remains: it is easy to misinterpret the notion of "alignment of the Self with the ego". This is because from an ego standpoint, the Self is always aligned (two non-identical points always form a straight line). This is where the viewer's role is critical: it is only through a triangulation – between viewer, ego and Self – that true perspective can happen.

This requires the viewer's ability to step aside – albeit temporarily, punctually – from both ego and Self. Here again, it is this stepping aside, and the habit of keeping this distance, that can protect and improve your ability to decide.

ORIENTATION POINT

The analogy between the viewer of a painting and ourselves as decision-makers shows the importance of adopting a central position. This seems obvious when admiring a work of art. Yet sometimes, when making decisions, our mind is preoccupied with too many external considerations, and we channel in other people's priorities and choices without realizing we are doing so, at the cost of the integrity of our own decisions. To step out from the ego to question where it is in relation to the Self, and therefore to the decision in hand, is always worthwhile.

In a strange way, by taking our place in the distance, away from both Self and ego, we are narrowing the gap with both: adopting a position is already and in itself reducing the distance. By default, if we do not take our place, this distance may remain infinite.

The best way to observe a precipice is to walk close to the edge. Similarly, the best way to contemplate the abyss of decision making is to step in close to the edge, from a position where we can observe the Self, and by so doing, get closer to the Self.

This movement was a key necessity of being for the German philosopher Arthur Schopenhauer. He expressed the view that man's suffering stems from the fact that he has distanced himself from the Will.

Granted, Jung's *Self* and Schopenhauer's *Will* are two different concepts. The Will for Schopenhauer is the original life force, and it precedes any representation: we are all, fundamentally, the expression of this one common energy: the Will to live. Schopenhauer's Will is not something that is born in each individual, but something that pre-exists the individual and therefore the Self; it is external to us and breathes through every single creation of nature.

This is different from the Self, which is the essence of each of us as individuals. Yet because the Self is so complex and will always remain a mystery, we can only observe it from the distance. Similarly, we can only approach the idea of the Will through approximation, through the trials and errors of experience.

Decisions demand a form of speculative affirmation. Deciding implies that we affirm something's place in the cosmos, its relation to other entities, in a way that can only be speculative because it relies on our blurred reading of the Will and our approximate understanding of the Self.

Therefore, decision making must leave room for chance – for randomness. Against the Western view that what is random is uncertain and therefore uncomfortable, we can oppose the Eastern view – for example, that found in Buddhism and Tao philosophy – that an acceptance of life's contingencies is a moral act in its purest form. This philosophy was a great source of inspiration for Schopenhauer.

To accept this part of randomness in our lives is not akin to resigning to chaos; on the contrary, it means accepting the principle of a higher order, whether we call it the Self, the Will, Nature or God.

Going back to Spinoza, if decisions are good, they collude with us to create joy. If they are bad, they subtract something from us and create sadness. The blueprint behind this principle is our inner necessity, because what is good for us, what brings us joy and elevates us, is what is needed by our soul. This inner necessity is therefore also a determining factor when it comes to our decision making.

At this stage of our journey, we depart once more from the standard view of decisions as the domain of facts and logic. After all, even Descartes accepted that if something is rational, it does not necessarily imply that it is true! Where this exploration has led us so far is the conclusion that decisions are essentially about an interplay: not between facts and logic, but between randomness and necessity.

What this interplay creates is a constellation of individual decisions randomly scattered but connected by the thread of necessity. Even in randomness, a thread exists. We see this in our night skies, where we have named groups of randomly scattered stars after recognizing a pattern – for example, Aquarius, Pegasus, Ursa Major and so on. The same way that our constellations are more significant than any single star, the thread between our decisions matters more than any single decision we make.

ORIENTATION POINT

We may find it reassuring to believe that we are the masters of our own decisions, and that we can apply our free will at all times. However, every decision involves a share of speculation, reflecting life's randomness. Besides, our choices are also guided by our inner necessity. In this alternative view of decisions, the key talent we seek is not the application of absolute rigour and pure logic. Instead, it is the agility to navigate through a different space, structured around randomness and the inner drives that move us.

CHAPTER 11
THE THREAD BETWEEN OUR DECISIONS

The myth of Ariadne is well known. Following the victory by King Minos of Crete over Athens, he condemns the vanquished to regularly send to him a group of seven young men and seven young women, to be fed to the Minotaur, a monstrous creature that is half-man, half-bull. One year, Theseus, son of the Athenian King Aegeus, volunteers to be one of the seven men, with the firm intention of killing the Minotaur. Upon landing in Crete, Theseus catches the eye of King Minos's daughter, Ariadne, who immediately falls in love with him. Betraying her father, she then helps Theseus by giving him a sword and a ball of thread, the latter to enable him to retrace an escape route back through the Labyrinth, the Minotaur's lair.

It is worth noting that the thread that Ariadne provides was originally meant for a different use, namely to help vessels navigate their way through tight passages.

In the myth, the thread has two specific functions: to navigate through tight passages, and to provide "real time" positioning (Ariadne holds one end of the thread, Theseus the other, and the thread indicates to her through its movements that he is still alive, in addition to pointing to his exact location).

If we now follow the *thread* of this analogy, it appears that what helps us to make difficult decisions (that is, navigate through tight passages) is also what reveals to us where we are.

The thread of decision making is our own GPS system.

These days, many taxi drivers in my home city of London rely on a GPS system called Waze. They claim it is more precise than other applications. The main reason? According to them, Waze relies on real-time input from drivers, private and professional alike, to update its advice on the fastest route to take you from A to B. So, if you take the shortest route but find it congested, you are informing the central software, which alerts all users to the fact that the longer route is now the quickest.

The thread is more important than individual decisions. The latter only serve to make the thread more reliable. In the words of the 18th-century poet Alexander Pope, "no one should be ashamed to admit they are wrong, which is but saying, in other words, that they are wiser today than they were yesterday."

Returning to the myth of the Minotaur, the expression "Ariadne's thread" is used nowadays in logic and, in particular, in artificial intelligence. It refers to the method by which we keep track of wrong paths, so that when faced with similar choices again we are encouraged to pick another option. In that world of applied logic, Ariadne's thread is close to the concept of "trial and error".

If there is no such thing as a wrong decision, we can conclude that all decisions are equally useful, in that they inform our understanding of the thread, thereby strengthening it.

We could even argue that decisions that are not conclusive may be more useful than the more "successful" ones, as they are more likely to question us; whereas successful decisions can sometimes be credited as being "right", despite resulting from factors outside our control.

In the words of the jazz musician Miles Davis, "It's not the note you play that's the wrong note – it's the note you play afterwards that makes it right or wrong."

Let us move from jazz to sports. Recently one of my clients was talking about the tennis champion Roger Federer, his all-time hero, in these words: "in many ways, you could say that Federer is a loser. Simply because he has lost many more championship matches than he has won!" What matters most is not whether we fall, but how we bounce back. Federer would simply never have become the champion he is, if he had not lost the matches he has lost and learnt from each experience. And the same is true of all other champions.

It follows that our lives, as decision-makers, should not be viewed as a binary succession of outcomes – some positive, some negative – accompanied by unavoidable moral judgements on each of them.

Gilles Deleuze, in his essay on Spinoza, wrote: "Existence is a test. But it is a physical or chemical test, an experimentation, the contrary of a Judgement." What he means is that the ultimate goal of our existence is not measured by the outcome of our actions, but by the effect of our actions. This is not about any judgement of success versus failure. It is all about the almost chemical effect that our thoughts and actions have on us and others: do they collude to create a greater whole, which elevates us and brings joy;

or do they destroy connections internally or externally and enslave us to external circumstances?

Moreover, in pursuing a life of elevation, are we doing this fully and with due intensity? In this context, trial and error does not mean we either succeed or fail: even an error can elevate us, through the greater awareness we gain from it. Federer is, after all, a world champion and a loser!

This entire process happens necessarily beyond good and evil, to use Nietzsche's expression, and also beyond judgement. It is similar to the study of dreams. No analyst would ever comment on a dream being right or wrong, or even good or bad. All dreams are useful in that they reveal or confirm one aspect of our psyche; and they also operate as compensation for the life that is unlived in the conscious world. (This, by the way, reminds me of the Surrealist artists' mission of creating "art without consciousness".)

Both dreams and Surreal art are media we use as compensation chambers, to reveal something about our Selves to ourselves. They provide an approximation of the Self. Through them, we get a little closer to the Self, even if it is bound to remain a mystery.

Our decisions have the same effect. Albert Camus wrote that "Life is the sum of all our choices." Or, to put the matter less catchily but more accurately, life is the sum of the absolute values of our choices. In our everyday world, where we count in relative values, a gain and a loss of the same value add up to zero. Absolute values are different. A negative number is treated as a positive. So, the sum of A and −A is not zero but 2 x A. It is time we started counting our decisions as absolutes.

ORIENTATION POINT

If we give up, even temporarily, the belief that decisions are either right or wrong, negative or positive, we open a window to a new way of life. Here, our approach to the outcomes of decisions is neutral, what matters is the effect they have on us. Sometimes, what may look like a "wrong" outcome (such as failing an exam) may point us in the direction of a true vocation. Even if the immediate outcome can be viewed as negative, the ultimate effect may be ideal. The same is true of decisions. What matters most is the thread between them, how they are connected and how each decision builds on the body of experience we have acquired in our lifetime to date.

CHAPTER 12

ENGAGING WITH THE FLOW OF THE WILL

"The future has several names. For the weak, it is impossible; for the fainthearted, it is unknown; but for the valiant, it is ideal."

Victor Hugo, *Deeds and Words*, 1875

If we accept that life is the absolute (as opposed to the relative) sum of the decisions we make, there should be no room for procrastination. This is because every decision either leads to an immediately positive outcome, or to an outcome we may perceive as negative but which nonetheless creates awareness of a flaw in our decision making. Often, the latter type of outcome will also carry with it – or point to – its own remedy.

Decisions, as part of the thread, reveal either our distance from the thread or our alignment with it. Both are equally useful.

You can decide to do, to get, to become anything you set your mind to. There's no guarantee you will succeed, or that your wishes will be realized; but this means that, over time, the decisions you make will become more tuned in to your true Self. And if you fail occasionally, this is the sign that you have stretched yourself outside your comfort zone, which is exactly the space you should be exploring. Welcome "misses" (rather than failures) are a likely sign you are aiming high, and that you find yourself on the right path.

In this context, procrastination equates to a negation of time. Procrastination assumes that if I don't choose today between options A and B, I will be able to choose tomorrow between the same options, as shown in the graphic on the following page:

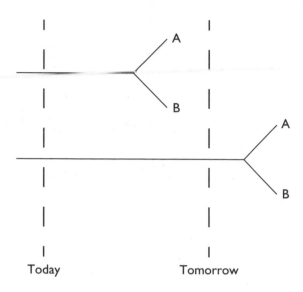

This assumption, already explored in Part I, needs to be revisited:

I am never faced with the choice between only options A and B. There is always an option C, which is "don't choose now". Therefore, if I don't choose either A or B, consciously or not I have chosen option C. Come tomorrow, A and B will exist no longer. I may live under the illusion that these options are still available, but because the conditions behind "A leading to a given outcome" will have changed, the likely outcome will also have changed. Therefore, A and B will become D and E, and come tomorrow, the choice ahead of me will be a different one (even if the propositions sound similar). We could even argue that option C (procrastination) will also have disappeared, and that procrastinating, because of tomorrow's different environment, should now be called option F (see the extended graphic opposite).

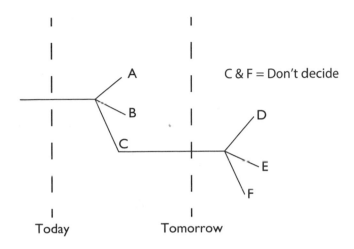

Let us take an example. Imagine you are invited to a friend's birthday party taking place in three months' time, and on the same day you are also expected to attend an important family function in another part of the country. It feels like a case of split loyalty, so you procrastinate, waiting a month to reply to either invitation.

You may feel that the choice between option A and option B is still the same choice, even though you are making it four weeks down the road. However, some things will have changed. Your lack of spontaneity will have affected people's reactions to your reply (whether you accept either invitation or not), and it will probably have affected your own feelings and attitude on the day. A and B have become D and E.

This highlights the significance of engaging with the flow, when making decisions.

Over the past 20 years, I have noticed that my most successful clients tend to be those who are fully engaged in a permanent flow of decision and activity. In their world, one thing always leads to another, without any stress necessarily intruding into their lives, but on the contrary in a highly organized, efficient and natural way. This does not only happen at work. It seems that even their holidays perfectly fulfil their intended goal of unwinding – something they can also achieve with great dedication!

This observation does not only apply to company chief executives. Friedrich Nietzsche was a strong believer in such total engagement with the Will. Prior to him, Schopenhauer had been more sceptical. He had expressed strong doubts that we can remain fully engaged with the Will. He suspected that if we follow the Will, we may soon start losing interest, as the Will requires us to constantly chase after new pursuits. As he famously wrote, "Life swings like a pendulum backward and forward between pain and boredom."

But let us not dismiss this view under the pretext that it sounds predictably pessimistic.

As we saw earlier (see page 145), in Schopenhauer's view the Will does not originate from within: it is an external force. Seeking the Will within us is therefore a doomed quest. I will never be able to identify from within what I truly want.

Schopenhauer also expresses the view that truth is always a relation between a judgement and something external to that judgement; and hence there is a fundamental contradiction in the notion of an "intrinsic truth".

For this reason, Schopenhauer assigns a pre-eminent role to human intelligence, as the part of us that serves the tendencies that emanate from the Will. Intelligence for Schopenhauer is primarily a sort of radar that identifies where the Will may appear, in order to track the direction in which it is headed.

To use another analogy, if Schopenhauer's Will is like a strong river cascading down a valley, it falls upon us to engage with the flow, throw the white-water rafts of our volition upon it, and assess the speed with which we must engage with it.

This is reminiscent of Gilles Deleuze's commentary on Spinoza. "It is by speed and slowness that one slips among things, that one connects with something else. One never commences; one never has a *tabula rasa*; one slips in, enters in the middle; one takes up or lays down rhythms."

How do we reconcile Schopenhauer's apparent contradiction between the need for our intelligence to be engaged with the Will and his doubts regarding our ability to remain engaged with it?

Here again, we find an answer in Spinoza's works, as he was a great influence on Schopenhauer. Spinoza expressed the view that there is not one volition, but many volitions. "There is in the mind no absolute faculty of positive or negative volition, but only particular volitions, such as this or that affirmation, and this or that negation".

In other words, our inability to remain permanently engaged with the Will is a non-issue, so long as we remain alert to the opportunities to serve the tendencies emanating from the Will, and each time apply ourselves through a separate, individual volition. What we need is permanent alertness, rather than permanent engagement.

This leads us to another paradox. On the one hand, we have already established that individual decisions are not an end for us: the thread is more important than individual decisions. And no decision is an end in and of itself, because every decision is always part judgement, part something external.

On the other hand, decisions are final for themselves, in that they possess an internal logic. A decision that does not complete its course through action is hardly worth taking. It is, therefore, our duty not only to take decisions but to take them to their logical end. This reminds me of those words from the *Ethics of the Fathers*: "You are not obligated to complete the work, but neither are you free to desist from it."

What comes out of this tension inherent in the paradox that decisions are not an end in themselves yet are final for themselves?

I believe that the answer to the above question lies in our unique role as humans. Our role is to manage the tension between what decisions are for, and what they are for us.

The thread of our decisions reveals the extent and frequency of our connection (or lack of connection) with the Will. The Will is pure essence: it has no tangible existence. Still, our decisions reveal the Will, rather in the way that a police inspector reveals fingerprints by brushing magnetic powder on an object.

Our decisions reveal the Will, not just through our immediate proximity to it but somehow, and even more powerfully, through our distance from it. The thread is both the means and the imprint of our connection with the Will.

This still leaves the question of how we should attempt to engage with the flow, at times when we are stuck – either procrastinating on the river bank or with our feet deeply anchored in the mud.

This scenario may befall us when facing our most difficult decisions. Nothing we have covered in this book has yet provided us with a practical answer.

These kinds of challenging decisions could be regarded as "thrombotic". They have the power to clog the arteries of volition: not only are we not engaged with the flow, we are potentially blocking the flow.

Although extremely daunting, such challenges can also be wonderfully helpful. They give you the opportunity, if spotted early, to avert disaster. The "clot" these situations create is really an unanswered question: what is the decision behind the decision?

If, like Spinoza, we accept that there is not just one volition, but several, then it is likely that volitions will occasionally cross paths. At these junctures, it may well be that one pending decision is stuck to another pending decision, and until that hidden, underlying decision is taken, the other choice may be impossible to make.

What are the options available in this situation? The first and most obvious involves decoupling decisions – in other words, untying the knots that make one decision dependent on another.

A simple example of this is what happens when we cannot decide where to go on a holiday, and at the same time when to go so that it least disrupts our professional or other obligations. This may lead to the status quo and no holiday in the end! The only solution is to treat each decision separately, starting with the higher-priority one.

What if we fail? What if despite all our best efforts, the two decisions are so entangled into each other that they cannot be decoupled? Then we must come to the realization that one thread, possibly two threads (each of them carrying one of the two unresolved decisions), may have come to an end. In other words, we may have to accept that it is time to think differently, to set our sights on something else entirely, to follow another direction. Perhaps this is the end of an ambition, a vision, a path. This is very different from an admission of defeat. It can only happen if we have genuinely committed our best efforts to resolving the conflict between the two paths that are so entangled. Sometimes, it may not even be possible to disentangle ourselves, because of our essential duties to others. But we owe it to ourselves to at least explore such possibilities.

ORIENTATION POINT

Our decisions form a thread, and this thread is more important than any individual decision. We need to engage with the thread, with sufficient momentum, or else risk being stuck in indecision. This does not mean that we need to be constantly making decisions, but that we need to be alert to the *opportunities* for making them. Even when we feel stuck, we have options. It may be we are attempting to follow more than one thread, creating a conflict we can best solve by abandoning at least one of them. Such realization may have the power to set us on a new and more positive path.

CHAPTER 13
OUR NARRATIVE

"We are such stuff as dreams are made on, and our little life is rounded with a sleep."

William Shakespeare, *The Tempest*, Act IV, scene i

The previous chapter ended with the acknowledgement that our volition follows multiple threads, and that these threads occasionally intersect, or even terminate together. (Loosely related to this is the image of a piece of fabric, the "stuff" of Shakespeare's Prospero in the above quotation.)

This weaving of the threads of our volition is akin to our dreams, in that it serves as an approximation to the Self. The Self only truly appears to us when we let our unconscious talk, in a way that our dreams can bring up to consciousness.

As true archaeologists of volition, let us put this "stuff" to the test, starting with the equivalent to radiocarbon dating – that is, etymology.

The root of the word *stuff* is Greek: *stuphein*, meaning "to draw together". In ancient French, *estoffer* means "to provide what is necessary".

What etymology reveals is that the stuff we are made of is the outcome of our drawing together certain threads, according to our inner necessity, not according to an externally imposed plan.

This is reminiscent of Spinoza's writings, and the notion that things are neither right nor wrong, only good or bad, depending on how they obey our necessity. For this reason, if we want to draw and weave together the threads of meaning that make up our lives, we need to learn how to read our own necessity. It is tempting to look at the threads of our volition – these long strings of decisions – as the different characters we inhabit from time to time, and to consider the individual decisions therein as either "in character" or "out of character".

If a decision is out of character, distant from the thread, the question becomes: which other thread does it adhere to? Or is it merely an anomaly, belonging to no thread of volition at all?

An example of this is how people react when they find out about their partner having an affair, especially when it is totally unexpected and seems entirely out of character. Many would see an affair as the ultimate sign of disloyalty, and immediately start seeking a separation or even a divorce. So, the general assumption is that the character we knew was always fake, and that our partner is now revealed in their true colours, as deeply flawed and untrustworthy. For the psychotherapist Esther Perel, the situation is always more complex. Although she is far from condoning affairs, she also recognizes that some affairs are not necessarily break-ups and can be "make-ups" instead, if both parties commit to understanding what may have led to this situation in the first place. If it is truly an anomaly, rather than a deep trait of character, it can even help a couple fix their deeper-rooted issues.

Let us return briefly to the analogy with actors. They may be performing many different parts, and they probably need to do this to become great actors. However, what we remember from them is rarely just one role, or the multiplicity and diversity of their performances. What we tend to remember is a certain unique spirit they bring to their art, and to all the roles they perform. In the same way, we can recognize something of a particular painter in all his or her works, be they portraits, landscapes or even abstract pictures – not just *self*-portraits.

What happens when we draw our threads of volition together – all of us, that is to say, not just actors or painters? Through the weaving of these threads what should in fact emerge is a pattern – or, to put the matter more grandly, a new form of belief and awareness.

Exercising volition is therefore also an exercise in "Self-belief". I am reminded of the *scrying* of the ancient esoteric sages: scrutinizing a crystal ball or some other phenomenon to foretell the future. Careful attention to, and interpretation of, the patterns that reveal themselves are the first step toward believing that our life has a meaning, and that we are *for* something.

Similar to scrying, volition is primarily an exercise of Self-discovery and of Self-deciphering. We must not impose an arbitrary vision of our Selves to ourselves. Think of the warning received by Gilgamesh, following the death of his friend Enkidu, in the ancient Mesopotamian epic: "The life that you seek, you will never find." The Self is there to be deciphered, not invented. Otherwise, we will end up with yet another character, another mask, another variation on the theme of the ego.

A thought-provoking analogy at this point may be drawn from religion (significantly the word *religion* means "drawing together", from the Latin *religere*). In an Orthodox church, an *iconostasis* is a wall of icons representing (literally *drawing together*) all the saintly characters that make up the narrative of the faith. It also marks the separation between nave and sanctuary. This recalls the Holy Temple in Jerusalem, where the Holy of Holies hosted the Ark of the Covenant. This most sacred area, which could only be accessed by high priests, was separated from the rest of the temple by a curtain known as the "Veil of the Temple".

Now, an invisible veil separates the known parts of our personality from its most mysterious aspects. This is the veil between ego and Self, conscious and unconscious, the accepted and the repressed, between light and shadow.

The wall of characters that separates holy from holiest in an Orthodox church has a reverse side: the panel or canvas on which each character is painted – a thick texture of fibres or threads. Similarly, the fabric of our decisions, each woven in the service of the characters we inhabit, creates a wall that protects access to the Self, but is at the same time the gate that allows us entry into this inner sanctum.

With the Self, we are dealing with an essence, a concept, without a tangible, phenomenal reality. It is a powerful presence within our understanding of our psyche, our soul, our reality. Yet it is an eternal mystery.

Golda Meier expressed a beautiful reflection on this subject: "Trust yourself: create the kind of self that you will be happy to live with all your life. Make the most of yourself by fanning the tiny, inner sparks of possibility into flames of achievement."

Here Meier describes a realistic ambition: the best we can aim for, she implies, is not the Self, but merely a "kind of self". This is an analogy or approximation of the Self, and our inspiration in this quest does not stem from the ideal, conceptual world but from the phenomenal world – namely: those *sparks* of possibility.

It remains to be seen how we can transform those sparks into "flames of achievement".

The problem with sparks is that they are ephemeral. In that respect, they are reminiscent of stars. The act of seeing stars happens in real time, but any star we see is millions of light years away, so the odds are that it has been long dead by the time its light appears to us.

Similarly, when we observe the sparks of possibility, they have probably disappeared already. But what matters more than those individual sparks is the unifying principle behind them, which brings us back to the "stuff", the fabric, and the threads it is made of.

Where should we look for those sparks? Where does "the kind of self that you will be happy to live with all your life" reside? Here again, Deleuze – in his commentary on Spinoza – points us in the right direction:

> "The individual will be called good (or free, or rational, or strong) who strives, insofar as he is capable, to organize his encounters, to join with whatever agrees with his nature, to combine his relation with relations that are compatible with his, and thereby to increase his power. For goodness is a matter of dynamism, power and the composition of power."

Of all the encounters we organize, "to join with whatever agrees with [our] nature", the most important has to be the encounter with ourselves. However, we all know people who do *not* "agree with [their own] nature". How can we make sure we succeed in this encounter, and do so with dynamism and strength?

My answer to this question is that, since the Self is an eternal mystery, we should be sure to aim only for a "kind of Self", rather than the Self. This is not mere wishful thinking. Instead, it relies on our best self-awareness and self-knowledge to create a plausible working assumption, a blueprint for who we are. We should also follow Jung's advice and move on, at least temporarily, from the idea of a *belief* in the Self, in favour of the *experience* of the Self.

As we now set camp in this new territory of the experience of the Self, and as we dig into the archaeology/etymology of this concept, what hints can we find that will help us better understand our own narrative?

The word *experience* comes to us from the Latin *ex-perior*, itself originating from the Greek word *peirao* meaning "to try, to attempt." Our experience is therefore what we get out of trying, of attempting something. And *peirao* is the same Greek root we find in the word *empirical*.

It follows that our experience of the Self must rely on our attempting to do things, to derive empirical evidence of the Self's nature. Experience is *selving* in that it circles upon the Self from afar, and by this movement gets increasingly closer. It approximates the Self, rather than *analysing* it – since to analyse is, literally, to break something up into smaller parts, an exercise that would be doomed by nature.

Therefore, the experience of the Self is essentially about trying, not about succeeding. The notion of *peirao* does not contain any hint of the experience's outcome. It is almost as if the outcome were utterly neutral, as long as each experience informs the subsequent one.

These ideas evoke the image of a doctor auscultating an ailing patient. Auscultating is literally "listening to, attending to". This is pure experience. The doctor's scientific knowledge will tell her how to auscultate, and where to press; the reaction or lack of reaction from the patient will inform her of where to listen next; and in all this process the doctor's many years of experience will help her derive a clear diagnosis based on this quality of attention.

When trying to gain our own experience of the Self, what we are aiming for is our Self-diagnosis.

Applying the tool of etymology, we observe that the word *diagnosis* is made up of two Greek roots: *dia-* meaning "apart", and *gnosis* meaning "to know, to recognize".

From this we derive the notion that if we want "to create the kind of self you will be happy to live with all your life", the approach we must follow is entirely diagnostic: it does not start with a grand vision of the Self, but it involves constantly probing, constantly trying. This is about accessing discrete moments of knowledge, recognizing things that are apart, and whilst we do so, failing, learning and trying better each time.

Of course, this does not mean we should go about trying things entirely at random, otherwise our life might just as well be spent playing roulette at the Casino. Let us remember Schopenhauer's view that, even if there is a place for chance, truth is always a combination of something external with human judgement.

Experience, the act of trying, is not the adherence to a new religion of fate and randomness: it is the act by which randomness informs knowledge, and therefore judgement. Experience is that window we open onto the world, whereby we let in sparks of randomness in order to discern a uniting order among them. Experience is our attempt at creating pockets of order out of pockets of chaos inside a carefully delineated canvas. It is also what frees us to *be* in the world, allowing us to create our meaning.

What is the alternative? The opposite of experience could be described as *stasis*, a period of inactivity, of any lack of trying.

Jung reminds us there is a river called Lethe, which runs through the abode of the dead, the realm of Hades. This is the river whose name survives in the word "lethargy". But Lethe is also the river of oblivion. It makes travellers forget the past. It also makes us forget ourselves. Ultimately, it makes us invisible to others and to ourselves.

The right path is the path of experience. This is not the path of forgetting oneself but, on the contrary, of remembering oneself – or rather of re-membering one's Self. This is the path toward greater understanding of who we truly are.

What comes out of this experience? Essentially, it is a feeling, an intuition of the Self. There is a word that means (both etymologically and literally) the "action of pressing out a feeling": this word is "expression".

The experience we discussed is only worth living if it translates into expression. In other words, this experience is expression, or it is nothing.

Our narrative is both the sum and the summary of these moments of expression. It is also the sum, the *body* of our decisions. Our narrative is therefore also our life.

On a more prosaic note, I remember a few years ago being invited by a fellow dog walker to attend a session run by her coaching group on the humble theme of "finding happiness". As I had nothing else to do on that rainy Sunday afternoon, I decided to give it a go. There was always an odd chance that I might find even a modicum of what they were promising. I did not. But what I did find was great discomfort about the focus given to "finding your purpose in life". Today, even more strongly, I find this notion of "purpose" rather naive and delusional. The term is overly aggrandizing yet at the same time limiting. It is aggrandizing in that it assumes that, like Jesus, Moses, the Buddha or Muhammad, and any other godly or saintly figure, we were all born with a God-given purpose. But it is also limiting in that it denies humankind the opportunities of multi-sidedness.

ORIENTATION POINT

Understanding the threads between our past choices helps us assess each new decision, and how it reflects our character. This process is dynamic, as each new decision also informs our own blueprint for who we want to be. It helps us elevate ourselves through the medium of decision making. Only experience will confirm, each time and with each decision, whether we are on the right track. And our ability to express what we have learnt from such experiences is what gives meaning to our lives.

Instead of this misleading quest for purpose, I favour the quest for meaning. And our personal narrative, the sum of our decisions, and their expression which makes sense of our lives, is nothing else than *language in the service of meaning*.

CHAPTER 14
MIND YOUR LANGUAGE

One of the most meaningful questions is the one God asks Adam in the Garden of Eden: "Where are you?" Let us juxtapose these biblical words with those at the very beginning of Hamlet, in the sentinel Barnardo's opening line: "Who's there?"

We can link these two versions of the question to a third one, this time in a 21st-century animated movie, *Anomalisa*. In this film, the main character, a motivational speaker who has lost his mojo, is faced with this unsettling question from his wife: "Who are you?"

This alignment of three articulations of the same message – Where are you?, Who are you?, Who is there? – presents a linearity between the concepts of *space*, *identity* and *language*.

Through language, the space in which we are (*where* are you?) is also our identity (*who* are you?); moreover, the third question (*who is there?*) can be read as a combination of the two others. Its meaning is "*Who are you* when you are *where you are?*" These three questions are really one and the same.

What this implies is that language creates the space in which we are who we are.

Language is not a mere communication tool. As Heidegger explains, when Aristotle wrote that "man is an animal gifted with language", he was unlikely to mean merely that man can speak whereas other animals cannot. The emphasis of Aristotle's line is that man can only be man through his ability to use language. The place that man (in the gender-neutral sense) occupies within this space called language, and how man inhabits that space, define man's identity. Language makes man a man in that it enables him to extract "Being" (*Sein*) out of "entities" or "beings" (*das Seiende*).

In this process the entities are elevated from their singularity to a state of universality represented by Being. For example, if I speak of that tree in front of me, I am elevating the single unique object that is this tree to the universality of all trees by applying the word "tree" to it.

This movement from singularity to universality through language is reminiscent of a similar movement we observed earlier (see page 139), when constructing our own model of decision making.

Decisions are analogous to language. Just as language gives existence to something conceptual and universal by naming it, decisions materialize our ideal and essential necessity into words.

Spinoza wrote: "Let us conceive a particular *volition*, namely, *the mode of thinking whereby the mind affirms [...].*" If volition is an affirmation, language is the key to understanding its true nature. How we decide is primarily how we affirm.

For this reason, our work would not be complete if we did not carry out a final dig, an exploration into the language of decision.

The language of decision is a language of composing and compounding, of connection and linkage. We could call it a language of hyphenation. Read further, and you will understand what I mean.

On seeing "I" to "I"

In Martin Buber's masterful book, *I and Thou*, the philosopher expresses his view that the word "I" has two different meanings: either *I-That* (Ich-Es) or *I-Thou* (Ich-Du).

This is not just an abstract philosophical concept. I have found my clients can all identify with it, in the context of how they address their various counterparts. People can immediately sense whether they are treated as a "That" (an entity to be dealt with) or as a "Thou", a human being worthy of focus and attention.

The move from *I-That* to *I-Thou* marks the transition from a world of co-habitation to a world of relation. The fundamental point here is that the significance of the hyphen in *I-Thou* points to the possibility of a connection between "I" and another "I".

In a similar way, and based on our journey so far, we can add two other interpretations of the word "I": these are *I-Self* and *I-Ego*. As *I-Thou* and *I-That* represent the relation between us and others, the pair *I-Ego* and *I-Self* represents the relation with ourselves.

On "And" versus "Or"

According to the American philosopher Ruth Chang, we make a fundamental mistake when we assume that values (such as goodness, beauty, justice) are akin to scientific quantities, which can be measured and defined precisely.

In her view, this is one of the main reasons we struggle with hard choices, beating ourselves up for finding them so difficult, and assuming this is due to our own shortcomings. In her view, "hard choices are hard because there is no best option."

She explains that there is a fourth way to look at hard choices, if we do not identify the options merely as equal, superior or inferior. This fourth way is what Chang calls "on a par". When two choices are equally attractive but for different reasons, we become disorientated. However, in a situation like this, a hard decision gives us the *normative* power to create reasons for ourselves, rather than having to depend on external reasons to make our decisions.

Through the normative power of hard choices, "we create reasons for ourselves to become this kind of person rather than that; we wholeheartedly become the person that we are; we become the authors of our own lives."

Earlier in this book, I wrote that the Will is like a strong river cascading down a valley, and that it befalls us to actively engage with its flow and throw the white-water rafts of our volition upon it. When facing hard choices, it is only by throwing in the weight of our volition that we can create the momentum needed to progress. Otherwise we drift, or we wait idly on the river bank until fate decides for us – and waiting is no safe option (remember Carl Jung's warning that what we deny inwardly will have a tendency to come back to us as fate in the external world).

"Becoming one with the Will" is truly normative. It is through our identification of the right time, place and way to engage with the Will that we write the story of our lives. In creating, through accurate use of our volition, our own story, we also create our own luck.

Often, instead of asking ourselves, "Is Option A *or* Option B better for us?", the question should be, "Since Option A *and* option B are on a par; when/how will I throw myself into this decision, and make this hard choice, which will be transformative for me?"

Here we have convincing proof of the power of "and". As Carl Jung wrote, "wholeness is not achieved by cutting off a portion of one's being, but by integrating contraries." Normative choices allow us to achieve this integration. Another, more literal way, is through the combination of contraries, rather than the exclusion of one option in favour of another.

The musician Daniel Barenboim takes inspiration from both musicianship and philosophy, having read Spinoza as a teenager and been greatly influenced by him. His teacher, Nadia Boulanger, believed the ideal musician should think with the heart and feel with the intellect. According to an article in the *Guardian* newspaper, "He constantly refers to apparently opposing qualities, which for him are constructive partners: choice and limitation, emotion and rationality ... His love of opposites received further impetus from Edward Said, whom he praises for his revelatory construct that parallels between ideas, topics and cultures can be of a paradoxical nature, not contradicting but enriching one another."

Closer to home, when I was planning to spend time in Rome to work on this book, I mentioned to the author Martin Lloyd-Elliott that on this occasion I was not intending to bring my camera and indulge in one of my favourite hobbies, street photography, as I wanted to focus on my writing. He subtly suggested to me that this might be a mistake, because the creative energy I get from photography would transfer to my writing. I am glad – and humbled – to confirm that he was right.

Ultimately, the combination of contraries is both the sign and cause of our multi-sidedness, something to be encouraged in everyone. The other direction, one-sidedness, which for many leads to comfortable habit, can also lead to neurosis. As Jung wrote, "neurosis is the inability to tolerate ambiguity."

Although Jung had nothing against one-sidedness as such, he also considered that it can be carried too far:

> "[...] so far that the complementary opposite is lost sight of, and the blackness of the white, the evil of the good, the depth of the heights, and so on, is no longer seen. When we cling to persona stuff, or focus exclusively on sweetness and light, repressing all forms of shadow, we create a condition in which the inner dynamic flow gets stuck."

And "stuckness", as we discovered earlier, is the enemy of momentum, and therefore of volition too.

What we observe through these two discussions (of *on a par* and *contrary* decisions) is that the *and*-ity of language, this semantic hyphenation, is also an "ambiguity management device".

"Nobody can stand tension beyond a certain point, but a weak personality has an impatient reaction, whereas a strong personality can continue in the tension for longer," wrote the Jungian psychoanalyst Marie-Louise von Franz.

"And" is the word that manages the ambiguous tension between similar (*on a par*) as well as opposite options (*contraries*). But when it comes to our decisions even more ambiguities come into play:

• Between the fact that decisions are final for themselves and are not final for us.

- Between the existence of different options and the fact that my choice will be dictated by my own necessity.
- Between missing a goal and positively learning from that experience.

On this last point, Rilke beautifully writes that the way we grow is through "being defeated, decisively, by constantly greater things."

There is no pessimism here, but instead an uplifting sense of our continual development in the quest for our personal destiny.

The conclusion from this reflection is that the essence of what is normative about our hard choices is the hyphenation implied in all the above scenarios. Our hard choices are as normative as the tension at the heart of our decisions is acute yet sustained.

If the essence of normativity I have described here is hyphenation, what is the essence of hyphenation? Here again we get a hint from etymology. Hyphen comes from the word meaning "a link under", a yoke, something we submit to: this is a sign of *sub-jugation*. In this sense, a hyphen is something that connects us to something greater than ourselves.

Through hyphenation of language, and its implicit management of tensions between contraries, we are connected to something greater than the ego. Hyphenation is normative in that it creates a link to the Self. Through this connection, it informs and elevates us simultaneously.

If the "yoke" of hyphenation is present in the word subjugation, it can also be traced in the word "conjugation". This will sound terribly grammatical, but even this realization may not be such a bad thing. After all, *grammar* has the same root as the word *grimoire*, which takes us to the world of magic.

Even this may not be a bad thing, because what is magic, if not the power to transform the world through first transforming ourselves, using volition, the power of our will?

As Sigmund Freud reminds us in his *Introductory Lectures on Psychoanalysis*:

"Words were originally magic and to this day words have retained much of their ancient magical power. By words one person can make another blissfully happy or drive him to despair, by words the teacher conveys his knowledge to his pupils, by words the orator carries his audience with him and determines their judgements and decisions."

A language of verbality

The language of volition is a language of hyphenation, as we have seen. It is also a language of conjugation. This is why we now need to look at another of its dimensions: *verbality*.

In his *Philological Grammar of the English Language*, published in 1824, Thomas Martin writes the following passage on verbs:

> "The last class of definitions to be noticed, are those that define the Verb to be 'the principal word in a sentence'. [...] Perhaps, many of these ideas are borrowed of Brightland, who calls the Verb 'the soul of the sentence', for without this a sentence cannot subsist, since nothing can be spoken, that is affirmed or denied, without it."

This concept of the verb as the "soul of the sentence" was even more significant for many ancient languages, in which the subject of the sentence was not even a separate word, but it was implied through the conjugation of the verb. Where we say "I love", Romans would say simply *amo*, Greeks would say *agapo* and Hebrews *hohev*. The subject is subjected, subjugated or subsumed into the verb through the verb's conjugation. This confirms the pre-eminence of the verb within the sentence.

If the verb is to be viewed as "the soul of language" – the word that affirms and therefore expresses volition, and without which there is no meaning – it could also be viewed as "the language of the soul". As such, verbs affirm and express *the soul's* volition.

According to the psychoanalyst James Hollis, the verb's supremacy is in contrast to our exaggerated propensity to assign a name to things:

> "It is our natural tendency [...] to want to reify, fix, harden, locate the world, and pin it down, in order to control it. As natural as this need is, it may also be the chief source of our misunderstanding, our alienation from the world and from the mysterious energies that form it [...] While ego consciousness wishes images upon which to fasten, such images betray the mystery, isolate it, limit it, and therefore move from the world of verbs to the world of nouns."

This is the reason why, in the Jewish faith, the true name of God cannot be said or written, and believers instead need to use proxies, one of which is *Hashem*, meaning literally "The Name" (*ha*, or "the"; and *shem*, or "name"). The word *shem* is also found in another expression meaning "noun": *shem etzem*, or literally "the name of the essence".

It could be argued that when we use nouns, we are only using the name, the envelope of the essence, its outside layer, not the essence itself. The language of the essence is indeed the verb.

Again in Hebrew, the word for verb is *poal*. But *poal* also means "activity" and "achievement". Verbs are not an outside layer, an outer shell, as nouns are. Verb is both the act and its intended outcome. Verb is the essence not only of language but also – more specifically – of the language of the soul. This may be because the invisible link between act and outcome, to perform the magic of volition, is one verb: to will. "I will" is our only way of bridging the gap between contingency and certainty.

Another sign of the magical powers of the verb "to will" is to be found in its dual meaning. "I will" is a more profound expression of "I want"; but it also predicts and reveals the outcome of a future action when we say, for example, "I will move to a new home."

Could it be that in the realm of volition, where the power of our Will is at its greatest, there is no *double entendre* – or, rather, that the two meanings of the words "I Will" are one and the same?

In this, our final archaeological exploration, we will dig further into the source of all volitions, our Will, and aim to find an answer there.

Part of the grammar we learn at school, is the conjugation of verbs in the different tenses: past; present; future; and the rest. I want to propose the view that in the grammar of decision this model is erroneous. This is another sign of our reification of nature. Hollis talked about this when discussing nouns versus verbs. I believe that the same point can be extended to verbs themselves. Albert Einstein said that "People like us, who believe in physics, know that the distinction between past, present, and future is only a stubbornly persistent illusion." It is so much easier to believe that something happened, is happening or is yet to happen. However, the past-present-future structure is our reifying imprint on nature.

Deep down, we all know that a past event can still haunt our thinking and our decisions today or tomorrow. Similarly, the fear of a future outcome may undermine our current choices. The past-present-future worldview is highly permeable.

I suggest that a more accurate representation of how our verbs conjugate through time, in particular when we say "I will", also follows three tenses – one could even say three "tensions" – but of a different nature:

1 *Nostalgia of the past*
2 *Active form*
3 *Nostalgia of the future*

I will deal with these in a contrarian order, leaving Active form till last:

Nostalgia of the past

This apparent tautology is meant to distinguish this first tense from the third: nostalgia of the future.

In nostalgia of the past, the meaning of "I will" is akin to: "I wish I did". In this tense, we may feel we speak in the present or the future when we say "I will" as an expression of our volition. However, the truth is that this expression is laden with suffering, remorse or regret for the past. "I will" is not merely informed by the past, it carries the past within it.

"We are not our history, we are what wishes to enter the world through us," writes James Hollis. Saying "I will" in this first tense, firmly set in the realm of history, is a negation of our potential and therefore of ourselves.

Nostalgia of the future

In this tense, the "tension" is of a different nature. Here the expression "I will" means "I wish I could". It is tainted with the fear that we may not deserve or be capable of the outcome we desire. It limits our scope. It forces us, once again, "to walk in shoes too small for us".

Søren Kierkegaard wrote that "The most painful state of being is remembering the future, particularly the one you'll never have."

There is only one way to heal this pain: following the principle of active form.

The active form

Between the nostalgias of past and future lies this second tense.

It is different from the *present* tense in "conventional" grammar, as it combines elements of present and future. This is the tense of affirmation and volition. Here "I will" means "I will" – simultaneously in both senses, the expression of both a desire and a future outcome.

In the active form, there is no room for the past. The past has happened and can – at best – *inform* our will in the active form: it cannot *live* in our will.

In the active form, there is no room for nostalgia. Nostalgia means literally "homesickness" (*Heimweh* in German), the deep longing for home.

In the active form there is no place for homesickness, because the ego has cut all ties with Eden and has found a new home, centred with the Self. This experience of individuation creates flow and plenitude, not pain.

Let us remember Spinoza's concept of the *conatus* as the essence, not the external quality of things: "Something is good because I want it", rather than "I want something because it is good".

Here is the root of the magical power of the Will: we "will" things to be good. We make our own luck, our own life.

The active form is the only space where we can find a suitable *home*. Again, I'm inspired by Spinoza's view that "The good or strong individual is the one who exists so fully or so intensely that he has gained eternity in his lifetime, so that death, always extensive, always external, is of little significance to him." There could be no better definition of the "active form".

In his essay on Spinoza, the French philosopher Pierre Zaoui writes that the question we should ask ourselves is not "What will I do next?" but instead, "Can I decide to be able to fully live the life that I am living?" What this implies is that any difficulty we have with decisions – which by definition involve a future state – is essentially a difficulty we have with our present condition. Being unable to decide, we reveal ourselves as ignorant of ourselves, our affects, our desires. We also reveal our inability to accept what we have become. The active form urges us to embrace our present state, the only one in which we feel, desire, think, are.

Earlier in this book, we discussed the myth of Chronos, the personification of linear time. We referred to his traditional representation as an elderly man holding a scythe, the symbol of separation and cutting off, and also the instrument commonly associated with the iconography of Death.

At this final stage of our exploration, as time is literally running out, it is worth paying a final visit to Chronos, as there is more than one side to him.

One of his aspects is the figure of time that inexorably passes by, abandoning us to our mortality. Now, since antiquity there has been an enduring confusion – and, later, simply a fusion – between Chronos and the Titan Cronus (in Greek, *Kronos* – who is also the Roman Saturn). Goya famously depicted Cronus as a terrifying giant devouring his own son. Through this symbolism, it seems that Chronos does not only abandon us, he also puts an end to our future potential.

A markedly different interpretation of Chronos, already found in Plato's *Phaedrus*, makes him a symbol of the sacred Mind, the intellect, which is both pure and full (*satur* in Latin, meaning "full" as in "saturated"). It is tempting to interpret "full" not as "overloaded with knowledge" but as "complete", "whole" – or, to use the Jungian term, "individuated".

In this context, answering the question behind our every decision, "Can I decide to be able to fully live the life that I am living?", involves overcoming these three limiting factors:

- Lack of *knowledge* or *understanding* of ourselves, our affects, our desires.
- Lack of *acceptance* of who and where we are.
- Lack of *individuation*, which can either be the cause or the consequence (or both at the same time) of the other two factors.

As we end our excavation, having methodically catalogued the artefacts we have painstakingly unearthed, we find ourselves on the brink of another, deeper, more personal exploration – one that cannot solely happen in a book, but for which we must elect to become, at once, the archaeologist and the site of this future expedition.

KEY SKILL 5

HOW TO DECIDE UNDER PRESSURE

"The scope of a decision will also include the time we give ourselves to execute it." (see page 132)

Processing the wisdom of intuition (see Key skill 3 on page 96) can take time; and the best decisions in any case are often those based on a process. So how can good decisions be made under time pressure? In the workplace, in particular, deadlines for action may be tight, even at times hectic. When pressure comes into the equation, how can you be sure to make the right choices?

Time and stress

Time management comprises a set of well-known strategies: delegate where it helps; make to-do lists; prioritize carefully; do not aim for perfection when adequacy is all that is needed ... and so on. All this is familiar business practice. However, the pressure may become so intense that in themselves these commonsense tricks of the trade are not enough: what is needed is a new mindset for dealing with stress.

Stress does not in fact come out of the blue: it builds up from a number of factors that are present in the situation early on, but may be insufficiently noticed. One of the culprits is the tendency of individuals to be over-optimistic in order to please those they are dealing with. An insecurity is often at work here: if I do not make this promise, I will lose the commission to a competitor; or I will let someone down.

It is important when declaring what you will deliver that you:

- Base your promise on a realistic assessment of what is possible, given (a) the resources you have; (b) the scale of the undertaking; (c) the probabilities that certain variables may slow down progress.
- Build into your promise if possible a set of hypotheticals that allow you to extend the deadline or recruit more support (an extra cost) if necessary.
- Make contingency plans in the event of pressure building as a result of the (c) variables coming into play.
- Monitor the undertaking as it evolves; often paying for extra resources early on can pre-empt a more expensive salvage operation later.

To achieve the second point may be time-consuming in itself. But being openly realistic with your counterparts, however problematic for the relationship in the short term, is a more reliable way to attain your vision and build trust as a foundation for future business.

Correcting pressure's view

All the above is about limiting pressure in advance, but this will not always be possible: for example, you may be shipped in to deal with an already pressured situation, and the expectation that you will succeed adds to potential stress levels.

This is where resilience comes in. Resilience is the strength to deal with stress. However, this is not a matter of being strong enough to **absorb** the pressure. Pressure absorbed creates mental and emotional tensions that can warp your decision making. Fatigue and worry can be distorting lenses. The solution is to approach pressured situations with a mindset that is fully self-aware and able to see that panic will never serve you; and at the same time to **look after yourself**. Skipping the gym, missing weekends and family occasions, not meeting up with friends ... all these lifestyle impacts are a recipe for stress to enlarge and impair your clarity of thought, like a monster inside your head that presses on your brain as it grows.

It may be useful to think of the ability to detach yourself from stress as part of your job description. The monster analogy is vivid and makes a valid point. However, your job involves using the power of thought to reveal that this image is inaccurate. You can tame stress by refusing to demonize it. Any emotions it provokes should be recognized – but not acted upon. Instead, focus on your standard time management strategies (prioritize, delegate and so on) in the knowledge that you are thereby doing the best possible job in the circumstances. Make nimble decisions about how to move forward effectively. Only if you have the self-awareness and strength to clear your mind of emotional complications and focus dispassionately on the facts will those decisions best serve you and your organization.

CONCLUSION

TS Eliot, in "Little Gidding", the last of his *Four Quartets*, famously reflected that the end of our explorations will be to arrive at our starting point and recognize the place for the first time. So now we find ourselves confronting Hamlet's soliloquy, "To be or not to be, that is the question", and its earlier version, "To be or not to be, I there's the point." (See page 6)

This is where we began and where we end. But what exactly is this point that Hamlet refers to? What does Shakespeare's *poetry* reveal to us, at the end of our exploration? And if poetry is faithful to its ancient Greek root, *poiein*, and is much more than an aesthetic pursuit, but literally creates something new, what does Hamlet's question create, and what does it reveal?

Our exploration in *The Art of Decision Making* ended with the *language* of decision and the concept of *verbality*. It is therefore fitting that the first and last question posed here should be the choice between essential verbality and its opposite: *to be* or *not to be*. As we have established, this is also the choice between three tenses: between active form and nostalgia – both of the past and of the future. It is also the choice between Will and regression, and between desire and lethargy.

The verbality to which I refer invokes both subjugation and conjugation. We need to link up to something higher, in order to connect with people and things around us. From a psychological point of view, we discovered that this is about linking up to the Self, in order to connect with the world around us.

Therefore, the final question we need to address explores this ultimate synaptic connection. Synapses are the junctions in our brains between two nerve cells. However, synapses are also – etymologically – the fastening or clasping together of separate entities. The thread we are following takes us through a labyrinth of synaptic connections.

To discover what this means in practical terms, we need to take a final trip to the place where it all started: ancient Greece.

One of the most important archaeological museums in Greece is located in Delphi, in the middle of the country, and about 200 miles northwest of Athens. The museum houses an extraordinary collection of sculptures and objects donated to the Delphic sanctuary in ancient times. The Delphic sanctuary was the site of the holiest temple in ancient Greece, and home to Pythia, Delphi's famous oracle and High Priestess of the temple of Apollo.

Among the museum's most prized items is a unique large, carved marble stone, of ovoid shape, referred to as the *Omphalos*, the Greek word for "navel". If Delphi was the centre of the ancient world, the Omphalos was the point where everything converged, and from which everything originated: the navel of the world. For this reason, the Delphic Omphalos was positioned in the Adyton, the sacred part of the temple, near the Pythia's tripod. People attribute magical virtues to this stone: it was believed to allow direct communication with the gods. According to the American archaeologist Leicester B Holland, the fact that the stone was hollow suggested it was used to funnel the *pneuma* (spirit, soul) to the Pythia during her divinatory sessions.

Outside the Adyton at the centre of the Temple, on the walls of the forecourt, visitors were greeted by two famous ancient Greek aphorisms: *Gnothi seauthon*, meaning "know thyself"; and *Meden agan*, meaning "nothing in excess".

According to James Hollis, "it is well known that the inscription over the entrance to the temple of Apollo at Delphi offered the sage advice, 'Know Thyself'. But it has been reported that over the entrance to the inner temple, which could be obtained only after a rigorous spiritual apprenticeship, there was inscribed, 'Thou Art'."

Hollis interprets this as the sign that we cannot truly be, unless we gain deep self-knowledge – an inspiring interpretation, and the key premise behind psychoanalysis.

However, in the spirit of TS Eliot's spiritual quest ending at its starting point, I want to suggest another interpretation.

If the Omphalos is indeed the navel of the world, and therefore our starting point, the source of our meaning may not be self-knowledge but *being*. Only by being, fully and consciously, can we acquire self-knowledge and experience life in all its most fulfilling aspects – following the "golden mean", living by our values and priorities, being brave enough to see our mistakes as positive, and so on.

Because of the destructions of the Temple, first by fire (in the 6th century BC), then by an earthquake (in 373 BC), we cannot verify which word was carved inside the Temple – whether it was εἶ ("Thou art") or ἴσθι ("Be!").

Either way, the intention is imperative – an injunction to be, a call to live in the active form. It is extremely unlikely that, even if the inscription were εἶ ("Thou art"), its point was to state the obvious fact: that we are – rather than not. Otherwise, it would be an invitation to gaze at our own human navels, rather than to venture forth via the world's navel.

As we conclude this book, and with it our formulation of a grammar of volition and of decision making, we add to the notion of verbality (with its three tenses of nostalgias and activity) the notion of the modality of verbs (English verbs have four modes: indicative, infinitive, imperative and subjunctive). And the mode of volition is the imperative. It is imperative that we *will* the world, that we provide our necessity with an outlet and an expression. We suggested, a few pages ago, that verbality helps us achieve this through a combination of sub-jugation and con-jugation: sub-jugating to the Self through our higher passions; while con-jugating not only with the world, but also internally, with our other passions.

"Mankind is a rope fastened between animal and overman – a rope over an abyss. [...] What is great about human beings is that they are a bridge and not a purpose: what is lovable about human beings is that they are a crossing over and a going under."

In these words, Nietzsche explains that the combination of conjugation and subjugation, or in his words of *overture* and *going under,* is what is most valuable in humankind.

The composition of our passions, through this subjugation-conjugation act, this ever-evolving hyphenation, is the story of our volition. Lived with insight and commitment, with a desire to learn and to remember ourselves, it becomes the story of our individuation, the narrative of our life.

Our toughest decisions, painful as they may be, offer us a unique window into the world, both external and internal. The exposure to chaos they imply should not be feared but warmly greeted. This chaos exists in the world, perhaps as a mere reflection of the necessary chaos that resides in ourselves. In this daunting realization may lie our salvation.

"I say unto you: One must still have chaos in oneself to be able to give birth to a dancing star.

I say unto you: You still have chaos in yourselves."

Friedrich Nietszsche

EPILOGUE

"Take comfort, you would not be looking for me if you had not already found me."

Blaise Pascal, *Pensées*

Dear Reader,

At the end of our journey together, I hope that this book will have presented you with some stimulating questions, and possibly a few illuminating answers too.

I wanted this work to be thought-provoking, but also nurtured the ambition that it would be action-provoking. Hence this Epilogue, a few final pages where we take stock of what we have accomplished together, in this journey from Procrastination to the Deciding Mind, and to our smartest choices.

During this journey, we have covered and uncovered some rich ground together. In Part I, we explored the defences we put up, and the fears we experience in the face of tough decisions. Through the looking-glass, we observed that these fears mirror deeper fears about ourselves.

In Part II we moved from the fear of the implication of decisions for ourselves, to the fear of the implication of ourselves for decisions. Since we are all prone to hiding, we then explored each room and chamber where we seek refuge and occasionally get stuck.

In Part III we explored the momentum needed to progress from will to decision. This led us to unearth the full "emotion-feeling-thought-speech-action" momentum chain, and the dynamic architecture of intentionality.

Finally, in Part IV we took our archaeological mission toward *perspective*, a dimension at the core of most modern theories of decision making. This integration of perspective in our journey led us to create a new volition model, featuring the Self, the ego and Decisions as key protagonists. Having then identified the role of randomness in decision making, we came to the

183

conclusion that the threads between our decisions are more significant than any individual decision. And these threads also help us engage with the flow of the Will. We proposed that the fabric these threads create when combined together is our human narrative, and then we explored the role of language in this narrative. This led us to compose a grammar of volition, the language behind the magic of willpower. There remains at least one unanswered question: where do we go from here?

This question needs to remain unanswered because it is – and must remain – a live question. It is the "What part of me cannot decide?" question, not "Why can I not decide?"

By asking and answering this question repeatedly, whenever we face tough choices, we create a pattern of decisions, and eventually a pattern of patterns. The resulting thick fabric this creates is the substance we need to make a bridge over to the Self. Although decisions help us become better decision-makers, they also help us become more individuated.

In this respect, tough decisions are both the problem created by our lack of connection with the Self, and the sole component of the solution to the same problem. This is because, just like us, decisions are part chaos and part order – a constantly chaos-ordering mechanism. Decisions are both the knife and the sharpening stone. They are decision-making sharpeners.

The sharper our decision making becomes, the clearer the cut, the neater the severing. "Severing" literally means releasing the *sève*, the French word for "sap" – the tree's lifeblood. And the tree itself is a potent symbol for the psyche. The sap is pure essence. It stands for true meaning. This is a direct experience of the mystery of the Self. Decisions are severing – and severing is *selving*.

Whenever we decide, we throw an arrow in the shape of this one letter "I" between the two roots of the word, to create a new reality: *de-I-cide*. This deicide is far from blasphemous. Each time we decide, our action marks the demise of a false God, the kind of spirit that gave birth to our false self.

This book started with the question: how can we, as human beings, become better decision-makers? It ends on the different question: how can we, as decision-makers, become better human beings?

If, as we imply, the answer to this question involves us crossing the bridge to the Self, and creating the pattern of patterns that is the sum of our decisions – also our meaningful life – we need a strong metaphor for this. This is because metaphors are literally a "carrying over" (from the Greek, *meta-phorein*). In this case, owing to the scope of the journey ahead, across the bridge to the Self, it may feel like we need the metaphor of all metaphors. What could it be?

If *metaphorein* means "to carry over", there is a word we inherited from the Latin that also means "to carry, to load". Surprisingly, this word is "caricature". Our own caricature may be the best metaphor for the Self, and therefore the best bridge to the Self.

Is there not a risk, however, that by creating our own caricature, we end up with yet another less sophisticated, less complete character? This would then take us in the opposite direction to our desired route toward individuation!

Admittedly, there is no real art in the vast majority of those satirical drawings we find in the press or online. But some of them capture our imagination in a memorable way. For example, in the 1960s, there were some striking caricatures in the French and foreign press depicting General De Gaulle, which over-emphasized the size of his nose and other facial features to create an immediately recognizable impression of haughtiness. Caricature is not simply a rough approximation of reality, or the inferior version of a portrait. Look, for example, at the 18th-century artist Giovanni Battista Tiepolo. The genius of his caricatures was to convey with as few "traits" as possible the essence – the sap – of his subject.

We do not get to the essence by adding more detail, more definition: on the contrary, we achieve this by removing all detail that is not essential.

There is a story in some management and self-help books about the visit paid by the Pope to Michelangelo in the early 16th century, upon the artist's completion of *David*, his great masterpiece.

Different versions of this story relate the moment when the Pope, having admired the statue of David, asked Michelangelo about the secret of his artistic genius. Michelangelo responded by saying, "It's simple. I just remove everything that is not David."

A beautiful story, but unfortunately without any traceable foundation!

There exists, however, a letter by Michelangelo to the historian and poet Benedetto Varchi, in which he writes: "The sculptor arrives at his end by taking away what is superfluous." This is a similar idea, even though it lacks the impact and the pomp of the possibly mythical Papal visit.

This approach of chiselling away the superfluous in order to reveal the essential is reminiscent of the Apophatic theology, also known as *Via Negativa* or *Via Negationis*. According to this ancient body of belief, we can only attempt to describe God through exclusion, by referring to what God is not, instead of what God is – something that is ineffable.

The way forward, whenever we are faced with hard decisions, involves following the exact same route: answering the "what cannot decide?" question by chiselling off what we are not, and removing layers of the superficiality of our existence, in order to reveal, as if through a veil, evanescent glimpses of Being.

I believe that this iteration can create the pattern that is also our path. What we will find along this path is what we must endeavour to seek again … and again … and again.

Joseph Bikart

ENDNOTES

Prologue

p93 "to the quality known as 'executive presence'..." Research by CTI, 2012. "Acting decisively" was seen by 70 per cent of respondents as a major contributor to executive presence, ranking second behind the ability to exude confidence.

Introduction

p6 "Who is the rebel? ... he is also a man who says yes." From Albert Camus' essay "L'Existence", 1945.

p6 "if there were a Devil, ... came to no decision." Martin Buber, *I and Thou*, Bloomsbury, 1937, p37.

PART I, INDECISION, INDECISION

Chapter I, Paradise Lost

p14 "You see, gentlemen, reason ... that goes with it." Fyodor Dostoyevsky, *Notes from the Underground* (1864), trans. Ronald Wilks, Penguin Classics, 2009, p26.

p14 "The older such people get ... one day they will do it." Erich Fromm, *Complete Works*, "Zum Gefühl der Ohnmacht", vol 1, Deutsche Verlags Anstalt, Stuttgart, 1980, p65; quoted by Marie-Louise von Franz in *The Problem of the* Puer Aeternus (Studies in Jungian Psychology by Jungian Analysts), Inner City Books, Toronto, 3rd edn, 2000, p64.

p15 "Research by the University of Chicago and Duke University ..." Gunter Hitsch and Ali Hortacsu of the University of Chicago and Dan Ariely of Duke, as cited in Roy F Baumeister and John Tierney, *Willpower: Why Self-control Is the Secret to Success*, Penguin, 2012, p101.

p15 "The primary motive ... the yearning to return." James Hollis, *The Eden Project: In Search of the Magical Other*, Inner City Books, 1998, p17.

p15 "All peoples, past and present... never fully recover." Ibid, p15.

Chapter 2, Defence Forces

p19 "A London newspaper … Mono-living." "How to streamline your life like Mark Zuckerberg", *Evening Standard*, 28 January 2016.

p20 "So does he still believe … such a good proverb." Tim Adams, "Dicing with Life", *The Guardian*, 27 August 2000.

p23 "In my films … give them." Source: *The Daily Telegraph*, 5 July 2016.

p24 "Perfectionism is not the path … hazardous detour." Brené Brown, *Daring Greatly: How the Courage to Be Vulnerable Transforms the Way We Live, Love, Parent, and Lead*, Penguin Life, 2012, p128.

p25 "Similarly, the human individual … his will power." Karen Horney, Neurosis and Human Growth, WW Norton & Co., 1950, p17.

Chapter 3, Project Fear

p28 "a team of professors from Harvard Business School embarked on a year-long research project …" These findings are extracted from Ranjay Gulati, Nitin Nohria and Franz Wohlgezogen, "Roaring Out of Recession", *HBR*, March 2010.

p32 "One needs not to be the fool … prevents you from living." From Marie-Louise Von Franz, *The Problem of the* Puer Aeternus (Studies in Jungian Psychology by Jungian Analysts), Inner City Books, Toronto, 3rd edn, 2000, p118.

p34 "There is even a 'Cognitive Bias Codex' available online." See www.findaspark.co.uk/resource/cognitive-bias-codex/ (Algorithmic design by John Manoogian III (JM3), categorization by Buster Benson, based on data from Wikipedia. For the complete list of cognitive biases see: https://en.wikipedia.org/wiki/List_of_cognitive_biases.

p36 "For every 'yes' … bales of hay." Irvin D Yalom, *The Gift of Therapy: An Open Letter to a New Generation of Therapists and Their Patients*, HarperCollins, 2002, p152.

p36 "should two courses be judged equal … the right course of action is clear." Buridan's words are quoted in Joel Levy, *The Infinite Tortoise*, Michael O'Mara Books, 2016, p26.

p36-7 "if man does not act from free will … children, fools, madmen, and so on." Benedict Spinoza, *Ethics,* Book 2, Proposition 49, *Scholium.*

p38 "the richest men and women … financial crisis showed us." John Kay, *Obliquity: Why Our Goals Are Best Achieved Indirectly*, Profile Books, 2011, p8.

p39 "Of things some are in our power, … not our own acts." Epictetus, *Enchiridion,* Dover Thrift Editions, 2004, p1.

p39 "If you then attempt … not in your power." Ibid, p2.

p40 "mated in the deep … first to see the light." Aristophanes, *The Birds*, lines 695–9.

p44 "Why has [man] … the beginning of death." Fyodor Dostoyevsky, *Notes from the Underground*, 1864, Loki's Publishing, pp35–6.

p45 "the worst inferno … what we seek." James Hollis, *The Eden Project: In Search of the Magical Other*, Inner City Books, 1998, p61.

p48 "Living within a constricted view … our own largeness of soul …" James Hollis, *Finding Meaning in the Second Half of Life: How to Finally, Really Grow Up*, Avery, 2006, p31.

p48 "the values and strategies … our family and our culture." Ibid, p29.

p51 "As they denied…unyielding ice", Dante Alighieri, Inferno, introductory notes to Canto XXXII by John Ciardi, Signet Classics, 2001, p259.

Chapter 4, Through the Looking Glass

p58 "what psychologists Jeffery E Young and Janet S Klosko call 'lifetraps'." I have taken this material from their book, *Reinventing Your Life: The Breakthrough Program to End Negative Behavior … and Feel Great Again*, Plume, reprint edn, 1994.

PART II, WHERE ART THOU?

Chapter 5, Self Starters

p70 "According to the Jungian analyst James Hollis … in modern life." James Hollis, *The Eden Project: In Search of the Magical Other*, Inner City Books, 1998, pp29–30.

p71 "In every era, God asks every person … How far along are you?'" Martin Buber, *The Way of Man,* Routledge Classics, 1965, p4.

Chapter 6, Hidden Chambers

p73 "She did not know … what you will." George Bernard Shaw, *Back to Methuselah*, Digiread Publishing, 1921, p53.

p74 "This would be just like the first thoughts of Copernicus … and left the stars at rest." Immanuel Kant, *Critique of Pure Reason*, B, xvi–xvii.

p75 "*Intuition* is concerned with time. … in their present existence." CG Jung, *Analytical Psychology: Its Theory and Practice* (Tavistock Lectures), Routledge & Kegan Paul, 1963, pp11–12.

p75 "Every child is an artist… after he grows up." *Time* magazine, "Ozmosis in Central Park", 4 October 1976.

p76 "Zabelina and Robinson are two neuropsychologists … adult creativity." Source: *Ideastogo*, March 2013 newsletter, "Why you should have a childlike imagination, and the research that proves it."

p76 "The child is a uniting symbol … because one exposes oneself too much." Marie-Louise von Franz, *The Problem of the* Puer Aeternus (Studies in Jungian Psychology by Jungian Analysts), Inner City Books, 3rd edn, 2000, p110.

p76 "Whereas intuition … our minds are clear." See Thea Zander, Ana L Fernandez Cruz, Martin P Winkelmann, Kirsten G Volz, "Scrutinizing the Emotional Nature of Intuitive Coherence Judgments", Werner Reichardt Centre for Integrative Neuroscience (CIN) at the University of Tübingen, 2016.

p78 "When the meeting was over … he had to break in." Source: The Jimmy Carter Presidential Library. www.jimmycarterlibrary.gov/research/thirteen_days_after_twenty_five_years

p78 "decided to work … yellow scratch pad." The President's own words, from Jimmy Carter, *Keeping Faith: Memoirs of a President*, University of Arkansas Press, 1995.

p79 "In Tversky and Kahneman's research … remained identical." Amos Tversky and Daniel Kahneman, "The Framing of Decisions and the Psychology of Choice", *Science*, new series, vol 211, 4481 (30 Jan 1981), pp 453–8.

p81 "When making … needs of our nature." Theodor Reik, *Listening with the Third Ear: The Inner Experience of a Psychoanalyst*, Grove, 1948, p vii.

p81 "A few years ago … Radboud University Nijmegen in The Netherlands." Source: Ap Dijksterhuis (Professor at Radboud University Nijmegen's Social Psychology Department), *The Smart Unconscious*, 2007.

p82 "In psychoanalyst Anthony Storr's words … 'one of Jung's least satisfactory contributions'." Anthony Storr, *Jung*, Routledge, 1991, p77.

p83 "Aristotle's definition of virtue … 'extremes of deficiency and excess'.". Source: Aristotle, *Nicomachean Ethics*, Book II, Chapter 6.

p87 "The great truth … or simply accessories." Arthur Schopenhauer, *The World as Will and Representation*, Vol 1, Book 4, expanded edn, 1859.

p87 "of moving toward one's ultimate purpose, … for which you were created." Adapted by Rabbi Jonathan Sacks, *From the teachings of the Lubavitcher Rebbe*, published and copyrighted by Kehot Publication

Society. www.chabad.org/therebbe/article_cdo/aid/110320/jewish/Torah-Studies-Lech-Lecha.htm. Inter-Directedness

p88 "The depth of the programmed powerlessness is greater than the hurt of the abuse." James Hollis, *The Eden Project: In Search of the Magical Other*, Inner City Books, 1998, p23.

p90 "the advance and subsequent retreat ... 'all of a piece'." Martin Buber, *The Way of Man*, Routledge Classics, 1965, p15.

p90 "This is the term also used by Martin Heidegger ... the state of being resolved." Source: Richard Sembera, *Rephrasing Heidegger: A Companion to* Being and Time, University of Ottawa Press, 2008, p180.

p91 "In a recent interview, Pinin Brambilla Barcilon ... upon completing her work." Source: *L'Italo-Americano*, 9 April 2015.

p92 "When nothing disturbs me ... And suddenly it's finished." Source: *Gerhard Richter: Panorama* interview (www.tate.org.uk/art/artists/gerhard-richter-1841/gerhard-richter-panorama), Tate Modern, London, 11 October 2011.

p93 "I am all in a sea ... the sake of those dear to me!" Bram Stoker, *Dracula* (1897), Penguin Classics, 2004, p25.

p95 "By keeping quiet ... I thought I ought to." As quoted in Anthony Storr, *Jung*, Routledge, 1991, p88.

PART III, THE MOMENTUM OF DECISIVENESS

Chapter 7, Of the Essence
p101 "It is the same with people ... maintain one's balance." Source: Albert Einstein Archives Online (www.alberteinstein.info).

p101-02 "How much more serious ... that they despaired of Roman power." Livy, 22.61.10, trans. Mark Healy, in *Cannae 216 BC: Hannibal Smashes Rome's Army*, Osprey Publishing, 1994, p86.

Chapter 8, Decision Flow
p105 "being completely involved ... like playing jazz." Quoted in John Geirland, "Go with the Flow", *Wired* magazine, September 1996, issue 4.09.

p106 "whenever the opportunities for ... equal to his or her capabilities." Mihaly Csíkszentmihályi, *Flow: The Psychology of Optimal Experience*, 1990, new edn Rider, 2002, p52.

p106 "Csíkszentmihályi shows that ..." The discussion on possibility vs actuality of control draws from ibid, p60.

p107 "among people who reported flow ... is relevant for the moment." Ibid, p87.

p107 "A self-centered individual ... conform to those ends." Ibid, p84.

p107 "psychic energy is too fluid and erratic." Ibid, p85.

p107 "doing their best in all circumstances." Ibid, p92.

Chapter 9, Under the Hood

p110 "Our response to situations ... without need for deliberation." This passage partly quoted and partly paraphrased is from Antonio Damasio, Descartes' Error, Chapter 8, "The Somatic-Marker Hypothesis", Vintage, 2006, p167.

p110 "somatic markers may not be sufficient ... Their absence reduces them." Antonio Damasio, *Descartes' Error*, Chapter 8, "The Somatic-Marker Hypothesis", Vintage, 2006, p173.

p110 "dopamine is missing ... do not help all patients." Antonio Damasio, *Looking for Spinoza: Joy, Sorrow and the Feeling Brain*, Houghton Mifflin Harcourt, 2003, p66.

p111 "But the unexpected happened ... how hopeless and exhausted she was." Ibid, pp67–8.

p111 "perception of the actual body changed by emotion." Ibid, p112.

p112 "each thing strives to persevere in its being." Baruch Spinoza, *Ethics*, Book 3, Proposition 6.

p112 "We neither strive for ... because we strive for, wish, seek, or desire it." Baruch Spinoza, *Ethics*, Book 2, Proposition 9, *Scholium*.

p112 "Let us then liken the soul ... a painfully difficult business." From Plato, *Phaedrus*, section 246b, trans. Alexander Nehamas and Paul Woodruff, Hackett, 1995.

p113 "An affect cannot be restrained ... and stronger affect." Baruch Spinoza, *Ethics*, Book 4, Proposition 7.

p114 "No one can desire to be happy ... actually to exist." Ibid, Proposition 21.

p114 "The origin of all conflicts ... I will straighten myself out." Martin Buber, *The Way of Man*, Chapter 4, "Beginning with Oneself", Routledge Classics, 1965, p22.

p115 "Speak what we feel, not what we ought to say." William Shakespeare, *King Lear*, V iii 324.

p116 "the spirit of evil ... the meaning of life is violated." Carl Jung, *Symbols of Transformation*, Collected Works, 5, para 551.

PART IV, THE DECIDING MIND

Chapter 10, A Question of Perspective

p125 "From every point of view" and "to which side reason...stronger movement of the reason", Saint Ignatius of Loyola, *Spiritual Exercises*, in *Personal Writings*, Penguin Classics, 1996, [182] p318.

p125 "should be as though the centre of a pair of scales" and "to keep as [our] objective the end for which [we were] created", ibid, [179] p318.

p125 "a person whom ... desire full perfection" and "then as my case ... I lay down for another", ibid [185], p319.

p126 "I should look ... want to have observed", ibid [186] and [187], p319.

p128 "Professor Joseph Badaracco of Harvard Business School ... 'How to tackle your toughest decisions'." https://hbr.org/2016/09/how-to-tackle-your-toughest-decisions.

p130 "Beauty is a form ... fundamental rule of nature." Leon Battista Alberti, *De Re Aedificatoria*, Book 9, Chapter 5.

p130 "nothing may be added, taken away or altered, but for the worse." Ibid, Book 6, Chapter 2.

p130 "Let me tell you what I do when I am painting ... figure in the painting to be." Leon Battista Alberti, *On Painting*, ed. Martin Kemp, Penguin Classics, 1991, p54.

p133 "The first thing to know is that a point ... its strongly implied absence." Ibid, p37.

p133 "It is of all the rays undoubtedly the most keen and vigorous. ... the leader and prince of rays." Ibid, p44.

p135 "I would not wish to be contradicted ... the earth is ash-coloured." Ibid, p45.

p139 "It does happen with some surfaces ... the greater the part of the surface it sees." Ibid, p42.

p144 "It turned out that the distal goals ... self-efficacy, and performance." Roy F Baumeister and John Tierney, *Willpower*, Penguin Books, 2011, p70.

Chapter 11, The Thread Between Our Decisions

p150 "Existence is a test. But it is ... the contrary of a Judgement." Gilles Deleuze, *Spinoza: Practical Philosophy*, City Lights, 2001, p40.

Chapter 12, Engaging with the Flow of the Will

p156 "It is by speed or slowness … or lays down rhythms." Gilles Deleuze, *Spinoza: Practical Philosophy*, City Lights, 2001, p123.

p157 "There is in the mind no absolute faculty … and this or that negation." Baruch Spinoza, *Ethics*, Book 2, Propositions 48–9.

p157 "You are not obligated to complete the work, but neither are you free to desist from it." *Ethics of the Fathers (Pirkei Avot)*, 2.16.

Chapter 13, Our Narrative

p164 "The individual will be called good … power and the composition of power." Gilles Deleuze, *Spinoza: Practical Philosophy*, City Lights, 2001, pp 22–3.

Chapter 14, Mind Your Language

p167 "Language makes man a man … or 'beings' *(das Seiende)*." The concepts of *Sein* and *Seiende* are explored by Martin Heidegger in his book *Sein und Zeit*: "Being," he writes, "is always the Being of Beings."

p168-69 The material from Ruth Chang is taken from her Ted Talk, "How to Make Hard Choices", www.ted.com.

p169-70 "He constantly refers … enriching one another." Susan Tomes, *The Guardian*, "Notes to Self", 23 August 2008.

p170 "so far that the complementary opposite … the inner dynamic flow gets stuck." CG Jung, *Collected Works*, 14, para 470.

p170 "Nobody can stand tension … continue in the tension for longer." Marie-Louise von Franz, *The Problem of the* Puer Aeternus (Studies in Jungian Psychology by Jungian Analysts), Inner City Books, 3rd edn, 2000, p50.

p171 "being defeated, decisively, by constantly greater things." Rainer Maria Rilke, *The Man Watching*, 1875.

p171 "Words were originally magic … determines their judgements and decisions." Sigmund Freud, *The Standard Edition of the Complete Psychological Works of Sigmund Freud*, Volume xv, Introductory Lectures on Psychoanalysis, 1915–16, Vintage Books, p17.

p172 "It is our natural tendency … from the world of verbs to the world of nouns." James Hollis, *What Matters Most*, Gotham Books, 2010, pp 98, 104.

p174 "We are not our history, we are what wishes to enter the world through us." James Hollis, *Hauntings: Dispelling the Ghosts Who Run Our Lives*, Chiron, 2013, p 53.

p175 "The good or strong individual … is of little significance to him." Gilles Deleuze, *Spinoza: Practical Philosophy*, City Lights, 2001, p41.

p175 "In his essay on Spinoza ... that I am living?" I have paraphrased and translated this paragraph from Philosophie Magazine hors-serie n. 29, "Spinoza, voir le monde autrement", 2016, p96.

p175 "A markedly different ... sacred Mind." Anna Akasoy and Guido Giglioni, *Renaissance Averroism and Its Aftermath: Arabic Philosophy in Early Modern Europe*, Springer, 2013.

Conclusion

p180 "*Gnothi seauthon*, meaning 'know thyself'; and *Meden agan*, meaning 'nothing in excess'." These details come from Pausanias, *Description of Greece*, 10.24.

p180 "it is well known that the inscription ... there was inscribed, 'Thou Art.'" James Hollis, *The Archetypal Imagination*, Texas A&M University Press, new edn, 2003.

p181 "Mankind is a rope ... a *crossing over* and a *going under*." Friedrich Nietzsche, *Thus Spoke Zarathustra*, Cambridge University Press, 1883, p7.

Epilogue

p183 "Take comfort ... already found me." Blaise Pascal, *Pensées*, The Mystery of Jesus, 736 [89].

WATKINS
Sharing Wisdom Since 1893

The story of Watkins began in 1893, when scholar of esotericism John Watkins founded our bookshop, inspired by the lament of his friend and teacher Madame Blavatsky that there was nowhere in London to buy books on mysticism, occultism or metaphysics. That moment marked the birth of Watkins, soon to become the publisher of many of the leading lights of spiritual literature, including Carl Jung, Rudolf Steiner, Alice Bailey and Chögyam Trungpa.

Today, the passion at Watkins Publishing for vigorous questioning is still resolute. Our stimulating and groundbreaking list ranges from ancient traditions and complementary medicine to the latest ideas about personal development, holistic wellbeing and consciousness exploration. We remain at the cutting edge, committed to publishing books that change lives.

DISCOVER MORE AT:
www.watkinspublishing.com

Read our blog   Watch and listen to   Sign up to
our authors in action   our mailing list

We celebrate conscious, passionate, wise and happy living.
Be part of that community by visiting

 /watkinspublishing    @watkinswisdom
/watkinsbooks   @watkinswisdom